THE
EQUITY
EDGE

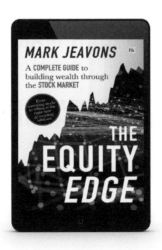

THE EQUITY EDGE

A **COMPLETE GUIDE** to building wealth through the **STOCK MARKET**

MARK JEAVONS

Harriman House

HARRIMAN HOUSE LTD
3 Viceroy Court
Petersfield
Hampshire
GU32 3LJ
GREAT BRITAIN
Tel: +44 (0)1730 233870

Email: enquiries@harriman-house.com
Website: www.harriman-house.com

First published in Great Britain in 2020

Copyright © Mark Jeavons

The right of Mark Jeavons to be identified as the Author has been asserted in accordance with the Copyright, Design and Patents Act 1988.

Print ISBN: 978-0-85719-798-6
eBook ISBN: 978-0-85719-799-3

British Library Cataloguing in Publication Data

A CIP catalogue record for this book can be obtained from the British Library.

CONTENTS

Chapter 9: Book Price and Valuation Ratios 95

Chapter 10: Qualitative Analysis 103

Chapter 11: Broker Valuations 121

Chapter 12: Long-term Fair Value 137

ABOUT THE AUTHOR

Mark Jeavons has successfully applied his quantitative skills and decades of investment experience to bottom-up analysis of stocks and shares using the system outlined in this new book, *The Equity Edge*. This has helped build a portfolio that provides significant income and growth and has helped him achieve financial freedom.

As a professional investor, he has also helped to manage large family funds (as well as his own personal funds) across a broad range of assets, including equities. He holds masters degrees in economics and in statistics, and currently works for one of the largest asset managers in the world.

ACKNOWLEDGEMENTS

Emily – this book is for you. Be happy and use the knowledge contained within to invest well.

I cannot express enough thanks to my family and friends for their continued support and encouragement. This book would not have been possible without them.

In particular, I would like to thank Professor Anneli Albi for her advice and encouragement throughout the journey of writing this book. Thanks also to David Jeavons, Steven Peake and Paul Cheng for reviewing the content and providing feedback. A special thanks to Ilona Szczepanczyk for all the creativity, inspiration and design work.

CHAPTER 1

THE EQUITY EDGE

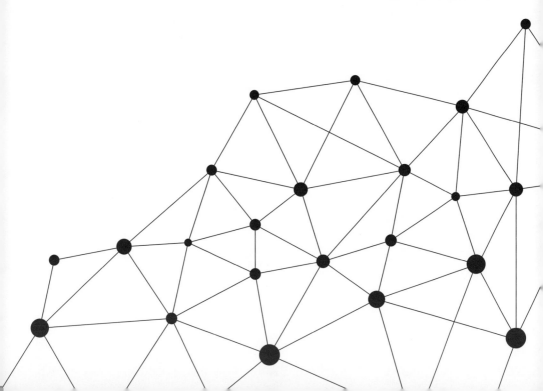

Introduction – Putting the odds in your favour

I F YOU WANT to grow your wealth over the long term, you need to invest. Common stocks – shares in listed companies – are one of the most effective ways to do so, boasting long-term performance that is hard to match. As a result, they play a core role in most investment portfolios.

But how do you go about investing in common stocks successfully?

What about beating the market average?

Can it be done reliably – and *safely*, with your wealth protected from risk of substantial loss?

I think it can. I have achieved returns of just over 15% a year; this is substantially better than the UK and world equity markets, which delivered returns of 5.2% and 6.9% per year respectively, over the same period. The superior returns were also achieved with lower risk of loss, with the largest drawdown on the portfolio being less than 12.5% compared with 47.7% and 52.8% drawdowns on UK and world equity markets, respectively. The approach I have used to do so is set out in this book so that anyone else can follow it too.

This is not the only way to make money from investing. But it is, in my view, a sensible, effective and enjoyable one – based on some simple and logical principles, and some easy-to-follow methods.

The purpose of this book is to set out this system and its methods in a practical, no-nonsense guide, so that anyone who reads it will be able to successfully invest in company shares, with the aim of achieving superior returns compared to the market average – all while protecting their wealth from the risk of substantial loss.

It is written for individual investors and entrepreneurs interested in taking responsibility for their own investing – and who value independent thinking and decision making.

I will explain how to implement my investment approach without the need for substantial professional help or years of specialised training. The system is designed to fundamentally improve the odds of growing your wealth by focusing on the key factors that ultimately deliver investment success, with good portfolio management to limit potential losses. This is achieved by taking

3

an analytical approach that combines looking at company numbers and key qualitative aspects that are good indicators of the future performance of a given investment.

Creating an equity edge

An equity edge is an investment strategy that allows a dynamic portfolio of shares to outperform the overall market over the long term. That is, there is an edge if the portfolio achieves higher returns than the market average with similar or less risk of loss.

The rate of return on your investments determines how quickly your wealth will grow. Achieving higher returns over the medium to long term means you grow your wealth more rapidly than the market – attaining a higher absolute level of wealth sooner.

The investment strategy described in this book creates an equity edge by using:

- focused business information analysis
- effective risk management
- market charting, which allows you to take advantage of underlying market price cycles.

Analysing key information to assess the strengths and weaknesses of companies and their likely return potential over the medium to long term can provide an analytic edge. Analysis allows you to draw informed conclusions about companies and make better investment decisions. Selecting quality companies that can reliably grow earnings and create market value over long time horizons helps to provide consistent returns. More importantly, avoiding the poorest companies which are steadily destroying market value helps to avoid losses and achieve market outperformance.

While there are many smart professional investors who can analyse the same information and reach similar conclusions, skewed incentives and different investment time horizons mean that the analytical advantage is not fully competed away. Asset managers are generally evaluated and compensated on their performance over short periods of less than a year. This often means that even if a company is very cheap, if there is no obvious catalyst that will cause the share price to rise over the short term, they won't buy it. It's therefore a huge advantage to be able to invest in companies that are likely to have the best returns over a longer time horizon.

The adoption of **effective risk management rules** means the risk of loss from a single company or from a widespread drawdown is limited. This ensures that your wealth avoids permanent damage and that you can recover from losses relatively quickly.

Drawdowns and volatility can harm long-term returns and cause investors to make mistakes due to behavioural biases. The rules are built into this book's investment strategy to help limit behavioural mistakes through systematic application.

If an investment continues to be loss making, the risk rules may eventually classify the investment as a mistake. Shares in the company will be promptly sold to cut losses, while money is reallocated to better performing companies. Conversely, when individual investments move into profit, some of these profits will be locked in, ensuring a gain can no longer become a loss. This allows portfolio profits to be run while losses are limited.

It is critical to manage overall risk to reduce time spent in drawdowns. Bear (or down) markets are a painful reality of the economic cycle and can devastate portfolio value if left unchecked. The risk rules naturally de-risk the portfolio in severe bear markets, such as the 2008 great financial crisis, by reducing equity allocations as the downturn begins.

By taking an agile approach, investors can enhance their compound and risk-adjusted returns over a complete market cycle using **market charting**. Market charting allows you to examine price movements to understand current price trends and where markets are in their respective price cycles.

When a market is trending down, company share prices tend to fall as market sentiment remains bearish. During these periods, additional purchases of company shares are put on hold while some existing holdings, according to selling rules, may be sold (to limit losses or take profits) – thus moving more of the portfolio into cash. This helps to limit short-term losses from a widespread market drawdown and ensures the portfolio is better positioned for a market recovery.

When markets begin to recover, investors can take advantage of improving sentiment and general upward market price momentum by reinvesting cash in high-quality companies. Such circumstances increase the likelihood of investments moving into profit sooner rather than later.

A framework for your investment decisions

The following chapters are structured to provide a framework for arriving at investment decisions and managing an equity portfolio.

The structure of the book breaks down the investing process into five key stages:

1. Selecting quality listed companies to invest in.

2. Valuing quality companies to understand whether they are fairly valued.

3. Timing purchases of company shares based on valuation and market charts.

4. Selling company shares using simple rules.

5. Applying risk rules to ensure the portfolio is well diversified and the risk of loss is limited.

These are all crucial steps in determining what to invest in and for how long.

Selecting quality companies involves multiple fundamental checks of reported company numbers, which can be used to provide insight into the quality and value of a company. These checks will help you to build an overall impression of the company and decide whether a company is worth investing in.

How to select quality companies and perform fundamental checks is explained in chapters 2 to 10.

Chapter 2: Screening for Company Shares

This chapter focuses on using screening tools to narrow down the list of companies to research, eliminating those companies with poor fundamentals. This leaves a more focused list of companies to research.

Chapter 3: Earnings Checks

This chapter looks at whether a company has reliably made a profit and whether the company is able to steadily grow profits over time. Normally you will want to avoid loss-making companies.

Chapter 4: Sales Checks

Company sales are an important measure of a company's performance and prospects. Looking at underlying trends in revenue streams provides insight on business efficiency, profitability and sustainable success.

Chapter 5: Cash-flow Checks

Cash flow analysis measures how much cash is generated and spent by a business over a period. An examination of cash flow provides a sense of whether revenues are generating sufficient cash to cover expenses, and whether stated profits are backed by positive cash flow generation.

Chapter 6: Dividend Checks

Dividend checks are used to ensure that companies paying a dividend will be able to reliably continue to pay the dividend and grow payments over time.

Chapter 7: Debt and Solvency Checks

A strong balance sheet can ensure that a company is able to survive a market downturn and has a low probability of bankruptcy. The debt and solvency checks help to ensure company debt levels are manageable and that the near-term likelihood of financial distress is low.

Chapter 8: Competitive-advantage Checks

This chapter shows how to assess whether a company has a superior business position based on the company's accounting numbers.

Chapter 9: Book Price and Valuation Ratios

This chapter discusses how to interpret book value ratios, as well as how to come to an overall view on valuation, based on a broad spectrum of valuation ratios.

Chapter 10: Qualitative Analysis

Qualitative analysis helps to build an understanding of a company and what they do. Leadership and the prospects of a company can be assessed, and the strengths and weaknesses determined. This includes major risks, which could have a substantial negative impact on the business (threats) and positive catalysts for growth (opportunities). This helps to further narrow down the buy list of companies.

The valuation of company shares is covered in chapters 11 and 12.

Chapter 11: Broker Valuations

This chapter shows you how to use broker views on earnings, sales and dividends to produce a consensus price forecast for a company over the next two years, as well as how to construct a price range the shares are expected to trade within. This provides a short-term consensus view on whether the current share price offers good value or not.

Chapter 12: Long-term Fair Value

This chapter shows you how to produce an independent, long-term valuation of a company's shares using a variety of methods. The estimated valuation can then help you to assess the possible returns that might be generated from an investment in the company at the current share price. You can then make an informed decision about whether there is sufficient margin of safety to make an investment worthwhile.

Strategies for **timing the purchase of shares** are covered in chapter 13.

Chapter 13: Charting for Investors

The use of charts and technical analysis is a valuable tool that can help you understand the current market and company price trends. This allows you to avoid price drawdowns and identify more opportune periods in which to invest.

There are three key strategies for buying shares at an advantageous time. Their aim is to limit the short-term downside risk and take advantage of positive price momentum, which makes it more likely that an investment will move quickly into profit.

Chapter 14 covers **when to sell shares**.

Chapter 14: When to Sell Shares

This chapter outlines some rules that can be followed to systematically decide when to sell shares. Application of these rules provides a simple decision-making process that can help avoid common investment mistakes, while removing some of the uncertainty and stress involved with making selling decisions.

Chapter 15 covers **risk management** through investment allocation.

Chapter 15: Managing Investment Allocation

Managing the allocation of investments within the portfolio is one of the most important aspects of investing successfully in the stock market. This chapter explains some simple allocation guidelines that ensure losses are limited, which in turn serves to help maximise long-term returns. Following these guidelines will help you to reduce the fear of a loss and avoid costly mistakes that can severely damage portfolio value.

Chapter 16: Bringing it all Together

This chapter discusses the day-to-day running of the system and how you can apply it to the share portfolios that you manage.

The resources and tools you will need

In order to analyse companies and follow the markets you need access to information. While a large proportion of this information is free, the tools and information that add the most value are those you need to pay for.

Screening and data websites

Screening and data websites select and gather quantitative information about listed companies. They provide a convenient way to research a company and assess whether it is worth investing in.

There are many free screening services, but screening criteria is normally limited, meaning more work is required to narrow down a selection of quality companies. My preference is to use paid services, which provide a greater selection of criteria – including more sophisticated criteria, such as indicators for balance sheet health, bankruptcy risk and earnings manipulation. These additions generate a more refined list of companies likely to be worth investing in.

Stockopedia

Currently, I use the screening service called Stockopedia (www.stockopedia. com). Stockopedia offers a range of regional screening services, covering the UK, US, Europe, Canada, Australasia and Developed Asia (Japan, Hong Kong, Singapore, Taiwan and South Korea). Since companies in the largest developed markets are covered here, the screening tools are suitable for most investors.

Alternative screening services

Other potential paid screening services include SharePad (www.sharescope. co.uk), Zacks (www.zacks.com) and UncleStock (www.unclestock.com).

While you won't be able to use them to fully implement the screens listed in chapter 2, free screening services worth checking out are: Finviz (www.finviz.com) and Yahoo! Finance (finance.yahoo.com/screener).

Morningstar

One of the main sources of company data, Morningstar (www.morningstar.co.uk), can be used to carry out detailed quantitative analysis and produce valuations. It covers most listed companies across developed regions. This premium service provides up to ten years of financial accounts, along with key ratios and metrics calculated for each company. The information is standardised, making it easier to carry out analysis.

The service also provides access to independent analyst research, including research on many listed UK and international companies. However, focus tends to be on medium to large companies.

Financial news

Financial news can be used to maintain a general understanding of the market, as well as keep investors informed of the latest developments in companies. Reading articles about what is benefitting or hurting a sector or industry can help you make better investing decisions.

The *Financial Times* (www.ft.com) and *Bloomberg* (www.bloomberg.com) offer a range of articles on the broader market and sectors, alongside discussion about the larger listed companies and events affecting them. However, these news sources have little coverage of smaller companies.

The Economist (www.economist.com) is useful to gain a broader perspective on current affairs. Main articles each week provide thoughtful commentary that may be helpful when thinking about what might affect the companies you invest in.

Company news

The main magazines covering listed company shares in the UK are the *Investors Chronicle* (IC) (www.investorschronicle.co.uk) and *Shares* (www.sharesmagazine.co.uk). Both contain commentary on small and large companies, and are useful resources to keep up-to-date on company news.

These news sources provide a concise, historic summary of company performance and investor sentiment – useful knowledge when undertaking qualitative analysis of a company (as outlined in chapter 10). Look for compelling investment stories within the magazines; if any companies you are interested in appear, you may decide to prioritise their further research.

Charting software

There are several free websites that offer share price charts. Most of them are able to replicate the charts used in chapter 13, where charting strategies are outlined.

My preferred websites are TradingViews (www.tradingviews.com) and StockCharts (www.stockcharts.com). These websites cover listed companies in most regions and have a large selection of technical indicators that can be applied. The daily and weekly chart layouts and indicators used in this book can be replicated for free using TradingViews.

The Equity Edge website and newsletter

The Equity Edge website (www.theequityedge.com) offers a subscription service designed to provide all the information you need to implement the analysis and strategies outlined in this book in one place, including company research and information on actual portfolios being run using the system. The subscription service provides access to research content, with a focus on UK and US listed companies.

Members receive a monthly newsletter containing market commentary and the latest company research and investment opportunities. Research for each company includes key numbers and summary statistics mentioned in this book, as well as commentary outlining our interpretation of the analysis and our view on the company. The current buy lists for income, value and growth companies are also provided, with links to company research.

Summary

Building an equity edge through quantitative and qualitative business analysis, effective risk management and charting can lead to superior returns to the overall market, over the long term, with lower overall risk. The following chapters present a detailed guide on how to implement an investment system that effectively develops an edge.

CHAPTER 2

SCREENING FOR COMPANY SHARES

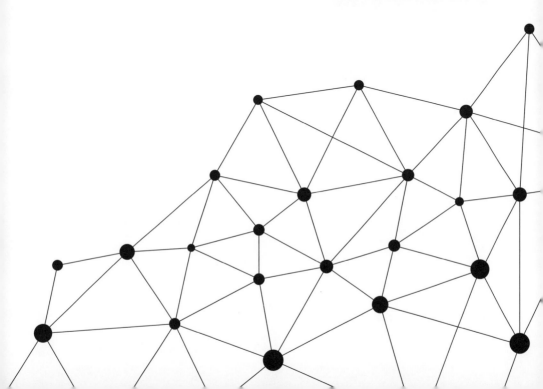

Introduction

I T IS NOT feasible for an individual investor to research every listed company in detail. A share-screening tool is therefore invaluable, as it helps filter listed companies into a more manageable list by specifying desirable fundamentals. Shortlisted companies can then be researched in detail. Through eliminating companies with poor fundamentals, you increase your odds of finding the best companies to invest in.

This chapter looks at a variety of screens that meet different strategic needs. The screens are separated into three groups: **income**, **value** and **growth**. Income screens are designed to find companies that provide a reliable, steady income. These companies are useful when company shares are held within a tax wrapper (such as an ISA), so income is not taxable. Value companies are companies where the fundamental value is likely to be well below the current price. Growth companies are companies that are growing earnings rapidly but are not currently overly expensive in valuation terms.

Both value and growth companies offer an opportunity for significant capital appreciation. This is useful when investments are outside tax-free wrappers and dividend income is taxable. Investing for capital gains is therefore more efficient (as taxes are not taken until the shares are sold) and it allows you to make use of capital gains allowances, which lower your overall tax bill.

In addition to these three groups of screens, an **economic moat** screen is provided. This screen helps identify companies with a durable competitive advantage likely to offer decent long-term returns. Income, value or growth companies appearing on this list should be prioritised for further research and investment. This screen can also be thought of as an alternative growth screen.

Income screens

Income screens are designed to look for companies that regularly pay out dividend income and are likely to continue doing so over the medium to long term.

Screen 1: Quality income screen

The quality income screen aims to identify companies with strong fundamentals and high yields. High-quality companies that have a high, sustainable dividend yield have been shown to perform well relative to the overall market, with good capital gains, low risk of loss and regular income-supporting returns.

The quality income screen criteria are as follows:

Rolling dividend yield higher than the average market yield plus 1% or 4%, whichever is lower

The dividend per share (DPS) is the amount of money paid out by a company each year per share owned in the company. The rolling DPS is a weighted average of the current year's DPS and the forecast of the following year's DPS, where the weight is dependent on how far into the fiscal year a company is.

For example, suppose the DPS in the current year is 10p and the next year the DPS is forecast to be 20p. Then, a quarter of the way into the fiscal year, the rolling DPS will be 12.5p (= 0.75 × 10p + 0.25 × 20p). Using rolling values allows a like-for-like comparison of ratios between companies that have different reporting dates.

The rolling dividend yield is the rolling DPS divided by the current share price. It determines the income stream paid out by a company as a percentage of the current value of the company.

The rolling dividend yield is required to be 1% above the average market dividend yield or 4%, whichever is lower. For example, if the average yield for FTSE All Share companies is 3.6%, then the required rolling dividend yield hurdle would be set to 4%, as 4.6% (= 3.6% + 1%) is greater than 4%. The average dividend yields for different markets are published each week in the *Investors Chronicle* in the 'Market this week' section.

Rolling dividend yield less than 15%

A company's share price and dividend yield have an inverse relationship – i.e., when one goes down, the other goes up. Often when a company has a very high dividend yield it is likely to be the result of a depressed share price, rather than the company's ability to produce generous payouts.

A high historic yield can therefore be a warning sign that the dividend payment is going to be cut or that the share price is likely to fall further. High-quality companies with solid fundamentals should not see their share prices plummet. This screen is therefore set up to rule out companies with dividend yields above 15%.

Rolling dividend cover above 1.5

The dividend cover is the number of times dividends can be paid out of earnings. The higher the number, the more likely it is that the company will be able to continue paying out the dividend in future years. For example, if a share in a company has earnings per share of £1.50 and it pays a dividend of 50p, the dividend cover is 3 (= 150 ÷ 50). This is probably a healthy situation, as the company is retaining two thirds of its earnings to reinvest in the business.

A warning sign occurs when the dividend cover is below 1, as this indicates that the company is paying out more dividends than it has earned; the company is either running down its reserves or borrowing money to cover the earnings shortfall. In general, the higher the dividend cover, the better for investors looking for continuing income.

Rolling dividend cover is defined as rolling earnings per share divided by rolling dividends and is interpreted in a similar way. The screen is set up to require the rolling dividend cover to be more than 1.5. This ensures that no more than two thirds of earnings are paid out as dividends.

Market capitalisation greater than £800m

Market capitalisation is the current value of a company as recognised by the market. Large companies are likely to be able to survive market downturns and recessions better than small companies. The likelihood of complete loss is therefore low. The screen requires that companies have a market capitalisation of more than £800m.

Improving balance sheet – Piotroski F-score is 7 or higher

The Piotroski F-score is designed to measure the financial strength of a company using available data from financial statements. It is named after a Chicago accounting professor, Joseph Piotroski, who devised nine criteria to assess the financial health of a company. A company scores a point for every criterion it meets. The points are added up to give the Piotroski score, a discrete number between 0 and 9. The higher the score, the better the financial health of the company.

The nine criteria are:

Profitability

1. Bottom line. Score 1 if net income is positive in the current year.

2. Operating cash flow is a better earnings gauge. Score 1 if cash flow from operations in the current year is positive.

3. Return on assets (ROA) is a measure of profitability, defined as net income divided by total assets. Score 1 if the ROA is higher in the current period compared to the previous year.

4. Quality of earnings warns of accounting tricks. Score 1 if the cash flow from operations exceeds net income before extraordinary items.

Leverage, liquidity and source of funds

5. Leverage is the amount of debt used to finance a company's assets. A company with improving financial health should gradually reduce its leverage. Score 1 if there is a lower ratio of long-term debt to assets in the current period compared to the previous year.

6. The current ratio is a liquidity measure that is used to monitor a company's ability to pay back its short-term liabilities (short-term debt and payables) with its short-term assets (such as cash, inventory and receivables). It is defined as short-term assets divided by short-term liabilities. The higher the current ratio, the more capable the company is of paying its obligations. The liquidity of a company is improving when the current ratio is rising. Score 1 if there is a higher current ratio in the current year compared to the previous year.

7. Shares outstanding is a measure of potential dilution. If the total number of shares outstanding increases, current ownership of the company is being diluted. This generally won't happen for companies in good financial health (unless they are intent on making an acquisition). Score 1 if the company did not issue new shares in the preceding year.

Operating efficiency

8. Gross margin is a measure of competitive position. Score 1 if there is a higher gross margin compared to the previous year.

9. Asset turnover is a measure of a company's ability to use its assets to generate sales. It is defined as sales divided by total assets. This can be interpreted as the amount of sales generated per currency unit of assets. If asset turnover

improves over time it can be a signal of improving financial health. Score 1 if there is a higher asset turnover ratio year on year.

Good quality companies should have good financial health and should therefore meet most of the above criteria. A Piotroski score of 7 or higher is therefore required.

Low likelihood of going bankrupt – Altman Z-score is higher than 1.8

The Z-score was developed by finance professor Edward Altman in 1968. It is a model-based method to determine the likelihood of financial distress: the lower the score, the more likely the company will become financially distressed. (Note the Z-score is not suitable for financial companies.)

The Altman Z-score is a combination of five weighted business ratios that are used to estimate the likelihood of financial distress. The ratios are:

1. X_1 = Working capital ÷ total assets. This measures the liquid assets of a company. A company experiencing financial distress will usually experience shrinking liquidity.

2. X_2 = Retained earnings ÷ total assets. This ratio represents the cumulative profitability of the company. Shrinking corporate profitability is a warning sign that the company may be in trouble.

3. X_3 = Earnings before interest and taxes (EBIT) ÷ total assets. This ratio shows how productive a company is at generating earnings relative to its total asset size. Weaker companies will be less efficient at earnings creation.

4. X_4 = Market value of equity ÷ book value of total liabilities. This ratio offers a quick test of how far the company's assets can decline before the firm becomes technically insolvent (i.e., its liabilities exceed its current value). A company with weakening fundamentals will become less solvent over time and the ratio will fall. This ratio is used for manufacturing companies.

   X_{4A} = Book value of equity ÷ total liabilities. This ratio also offers a quick test of how far the company's assets can decline before the firm becomes technically insolvent (i.e., its liabilities exceed its accounting value). This ratio is used for non-manufacturing companies, as it provides greater predictive power than X_4 when considering the probability of financial distress.

5. X_5 = Sales ÷ total assets. Asset turnover is a measure of how effectively the company uses its assets to generate sales. Companies with weakening fundamentals will likely generate fewer sales for a given asset base.

For publicly listed manufacturing companies, the Altman Z-score is calculated as follows:

$$(1.2 \times X_1) + (1.4 \times X_2) + (3.3 \times X_3) + (0.6 \times X_4) + (1.0 \times X_5)$$

while the Altman Z-score for non-manufacturing companies is calculated as:

$$(6.56 \times X_1) + (3.26 \times X_2) + (6.72 \times X_3) + (1.05 \times X_{4A})$$

When a company is experiencing financial distress, the above ratios should fall, producing a lower overall Z-score. A score above 3 is deemed to be a healthy company. A score between 1.8 and 3 is in a grey area. A score below 1.8 suggests that a company has a high probability of becoming distressed within the next two years.

High-quality companies should not have a high chance of bankruptcy. Consequently, the screen is set up to remove companies with an Altman Z-score of 1.8 or lower.

Company does not belong to the finance sector

Companies in the finance sector are excluded. It is harder to judge a financial company's earnings and their ability to continue paying a dividend. Consequently, returns from companies in the financial sector tend to be more volatile than other sectors. The financial sector is therefore avoided when building a portfolio of quality companies with high dividend yield payout.

Optional: quality rank is above 80

The quality rank is a composite indicator produced by Stockopedia. It blends a range of quantitative factors pertaining to company cash flow, profitability and stability, to provide a general score of quality.

Every company in the market is ranked from 1–100 for each factor and a composite score is calculated as a weighted average of all these values. The quality rank is then calculated between zero and 100 for this composite score, where 100 is the best quality company in the market and zero is the worst company in the market. The higher the quality rank score, the better the quality of the company.

This criterion aims to identify the best quality companies by requiring a quality rank above 80.

If you are using an alternative screening tool, you can replace this criterion with an equivalent summary quality indicator or omit it altogether.

Screen 2: Growth and income screen

The growth and income screen is designed to select companies that are growing earnings while still offering above average dividend yields. The approach starts by looking for solid growth and reasonable quality in key metrics, then selects the subset of companies with the best dividend yields.

The growth and income screen criteria are:

Earnings upgrades over the next two financial years are positive

The screen first looks for companies where brokers have recently upgraded their forecasts for the next financial year. Analyst forecasts tend to trend, as they often get anchored to their previous forecasts and adjust their initial forecasts cautiously in reaction to new events; this often means that initial adjustments are insufficient and further adjustments over time are required.

The screen requires the broker forecast for the second (financial) year to have been upgraded in the past three months.

Current return on equity (ROE) is above the market median

Return on equity measures the rate of profit earned by a company for its shareholders. It is defined as net profit divided by shareholders' equity (which is assets minus liabilities). It is therefore a measure of the underlying quality of the business as it calculates a company's efficiency at generating profits from every unit of shareholders' equity. The screen is set up to require a return above the market median.

Rolling PE is less than 20

The PE ratio is a commonly used valuation measure. It is defined as the share price divided by earnings per share (EPS). It measures the multiple of earnings a company's share price is currently trading at. All other things being equal, the lower the multiple, the cheaper the company's shares are relative to earnings.

The rolling PE ratio is the current share price divided by rolling EPS. The rolling EPS is a weighted average of the current year's EPS and the forecast of the following year's EPS, where the weight is dependent on how far into the fiscal year a company is. Using rolling values allows a like-for-like comparison of rolling PE ratios between companies that have different reporting dates.

Companies with a high PE above 20 are generally thought of as expensive, unless they have very high earnings growth. Growth and income companies selected using this screen typically have more modest levels of growth. For this reason, it is reasonable to exclude companies with a PE ratio above 20.

Rolling PE over the next year is below the market median

In addition, the rolling (forward) PE ratio is required to be less than the market median so that only the cheapest half of the market is considered.

Company is not overly geared (burdened by debt) – gross gearing less than 1

The gross gearing ratio shows how encumbered a company is with debt. It is defined as total debt divided by the book value of shareholders' equity, where shareholders' equity is the value of assets which may be regarded as owned by the shareholders. The higher the gearing ratio, the higher the amount of debt to shareholder equity.

A highly geared company is more vulnerable to adverse shocks, such as operational problems or a downturn in the economy. The screen therefore requires total debt to be less than shareholder equity by choosing companies with gross gearing less than 1.

Dividend yield is above the market median

The screen aims to find growing companies that pay out above average dividend yields. The current dividend yield is therefore required to be above the current market median dividend yield.

Company is less sensitive to market volatility – beta is less than 1

If a company is less sensitive to the ebbs and flows of the economy, its shares should be less sensitive to the ebbs and flows of the market. Beta measures the relationship between movements in the wider market and company share price. The screen selects more defensive companies by setting an upper limit of 1 to beta.

Piotroski F-score above 5

As mentioned earlier in the chapter, the Piotroski F-score is designed to measure the financial strength of a company using available data from financial statements. The screen requires the Piotroski F-score to be higher than 5, which signals that the financial strength of the company is gradually improving.

Rolling dividend cover above 1.5

The screen is set up to require that the rolling dividend cover is more than 1.5. This ensures that no more than two thirds of earnings are paid out as dividends.

Rolling dividend yield over the next year is expected to be above average

The rolling dividend yield is the rolling dividend divided by the current share price. It determines the income stream paid out by a company as a percentage of the current value of the company.

The rolling dividend yield is required to be above the average dividend yield offered by companies in the market. The average dividend yields for different markets are published each week in the *Investors Chronicle*. For example, if the average yield for FTSE All Share companies is 3%, the required rolling dividend yield hurdle would be set to 3%.

Note that a premium is not added on to the rolling dividend yield (as in the quality income screen), due to the added benefit of growth in earnings, which will hopefully allow companies to grow their dividends quickly. Furthermore, adding a premium of 1% would significantly reduce the number of companies listed in the screen.

Market capitalisation above £20m – illiquid companies ruled out

The screen removes companies with a market value below £20m. These companies tend to be riskier and harder (and more expensive) to trade – most investors do not want to own them. These companies are therefore excluded.

Value screens

Value screens aim to find companies that are out of favour with the market and currently have cheap valuations. These companies potentially offer significant capital gains once there is a favourable revaluation.

The value screens are based on work done by David Dreman in his book, *Contrarian Investment Strategies: The Next Generation,* which aims to identify companies that have low valuations with higher than average dividend yield. The dividend yield helps to ensure that there is a regular return on the investment and some insulation from falls in value while waiting for the re-rating.

Screen 3: Low PE screen

The low price to earnings (PE) screen focuses on the cheapest 40% of companies in the market with above average dividend yields, financial health and growth characteristics. The price to earnings ratio is used as the key valuation metric. The lower the PE ratio, the cheaper and the more out of favour the companies are likely to be.

The low PE screen criteria are as follows:

Cheapest 40% of the market based on the PE ratio

The screen orders all the companies in the market by their price to earnings ratio and selects the bottom 40% of companies with the lowest PE ratio. These companies are out of favour with the market.

Sales above £100m

The screen targets large- and medium-sized companies because they are less likely to suffer from damaging operational or financial setbacks. Large companies generally have a higher market profile than smaller companies, which attracts wider attention from investors in better times. Furthermore, the accounts of larger companies tend to offer more reliable growth indicators as the financial statements are higher quality and more information is readily available from investment houses and regulators. The screen requires company sales to be larger than £100m.

Low debt levels compared to the market

Debt to assets is a measure of the extent to which a company's assets are financed by debt. It is defined as total debt divided by total assets. The higher the ratio, the greater the financial risk associated with the firm's operation. In addition, a high debt to assets ratio may indicate low borrowing capacity, which in turn will lower the firm's financial flexibility. The screen requires the debt to assets ratio to be less than the market average.

Liquid assets sufficient to cover current liabilities

The current ratio is a measure of short-term solvency. It is defined as current assets divided by current liabilities. Current assets include cash, cash equivalents and items that will become cash, such as money owed to the company, prepayments and stock. Current liabilities are the company's debts or obligations that need to be paid within the next 12 months. Current liabilities appear on the company's balance sheet and include short-term debt, accounts payable, accrued liabilities and other debts. When the current ratio is above 1, the company has sufficient income to cover upcoming liabilities.

The screen requires the current ratio to be greater than 1, which ensures that the company can continue trading over the short term and is deemed sufficiently solvent for further consideration.

Profit margins better than the market average

The net profit margin is a key measure of how efficient a company is at converting sales revenue into profit, taking into consideration all expenses of the company. The higher the net profit margin the more efficient (and profitable) the company. The screen selects companies that have net profit margins that are higher than the market average.

Return on equity (ROE) better than the market average

ROE is a useful measure of a company's profitability as it shows the return being generated for every pound of shareholder equity on the balance sheet. It is defined as net profit divided by shareholders' equity (which is assets minus liabilities). The higher the ROE for a company, the more value should be created for shareholders. Companies are required to have a ROE above the market average, which indicates they are more efficient at generating a profit than the average company in the market.

Earnings growth better than the market average

The screen requires that companies deliver earnings growth that outperforms the market, so that they are gradually increasing market value. Current earnings growth is therefore required to be above the market average (as measured by the median).

Above average dividend yield

The screen requires selected companies to have dividend yields that are above the market average. The dividend yield helps to ensure that there is a regular cash return, which helps to insulate from (temporary) falls in market value, while waiting for a re-rating.

Exclude companies that are collective investments

Collective investments are funds that combine the assets of various individuals and organisations to create a larger, well-diversified portfolio. The focus is on companies rather than funds. Collective investments are therefore excluded from the screen.

Piotroski F-score above 5

As mentioned, the Piotroski F-score is designed to measure the financial strength of a company using available data from financial statements. The screen requires the Piotroski F-score to be higher than 5, which signals that the financial strength of the company is likely to be improving.

Screen 4: Low PCF screen

The low price to cash flow (PCF) screen focuses on the cheapest 40% of companies in the market with above average dividend yields, financial health and growth characteristics. The price to cash flow (PCF) ratio is used as the valuation metric. The PCF ratio for a company is defined as share price divided by operating cash flow per share. The lower the PCF ratio the cheaper and the more out of favour the companies are likely to be.

The low PCF screen criteria are as follows:

Cheapest 40% of the market based on PCF ratio

The screen orders all the companies in the market by their price to cash flow ratio and selects the bottom 40% of companies with the lowest PCF ratio. These companies are out of favour with the market.

Sales above £100m

The screen targets large- and medium-sized companies because they are less likely to suffer from damaging operational or financial setbacks, tend to have a higher market profile and financial information tends to be more reliable. The screen requires the market value of the company to be larger than £100m.

Low debt levels compared to the market

The higher the debt to asset ratio, the greater the financial risk associated with the firm's operation and the lower the firm's financial flexibility. The screen requires the debt to assets ratio to be less than the market average.

Liquid assets sufficient to cover current liabilities

The current ratio is a measure of short-term solvency. The screen requires the current ratio to be greater than 1, which ensures that the company can continue trading over the short term and is deemed sufficiently solvent for further consideration.

Profit margins better than the market average

The net profit margin is a key measure of how efficient a company is at converting sales revenue into profit, taking into consideration all expenses of the company. The higher the net profit margin the more efficient (and profitable) the company. The screen selects companies that have net profit margins that are higher than the market average.

Earnings growth better than the market average

The screen requires that companies deliver earnings growth that outperforms the market. Current earnings growth is therefore required to be above the market average (as measured by the median).

Above average dividend yield

The screen requires selected companies to have dividend yields that are above the market average. The dividend yield helps to ensure that there is a regular cash return, which helps to insulate from (temporary) falls in market value, while waiting for a re-rating.

Exclude companies that are collective investments

Collective investments are funds that combine the assets of various individuals and organisations to create a larger, well-diversified portfolio. The focus is on companies rather than funds. Collective investments are therefore excluded from the screen.

Piotroski F-score above 5

As defined earlier in the chapter, the Piotroski F-score is designed to measure the financial strength of a company using available data from financial statements. The screen requires the Piotroski F-score to be higher than 5, which signals that the financial strength of the company is likely to be improving.

Growth screens

The growth screens are designed to find companies with high-quality, sustainable earnings growth that are still reasonably priced relative to the overall market. The focus is on buying companies that are likely to appreciate over time, rather than generate an income. As discussed in chapter 15, investing in growth companies can be advantageous if dividend income is likely to be taxed unfavourably.

The screens look for companies with high growth rates that are better than the market average, but with valuations that are below the market, giving you the best of both worlds.

Screen 5: Zulu growth

The Zulu growth screen is based on a screen outlined in Jim Slater's books, *The Zulu Principle* and *Beyond the Zulu Principle*. It looks for small companies where brokers are forecasting high earnings growth and where this growth has not been fully priced in given expected future earnings. Small companies tend to be less well researched and there is therefore a greater chance of finding undervalued companies to invest in.

The criteria for the Zulu growth screen are as follows:

Price earnings growth (PEG) ratio less than 0.75

A lower PE ratio typically indicates that the price is cheaper. However, companies with high growth rates normally have higher PE ratios. Thus, just using the PE ratio would make many of the high growth shares look overvalued. The PEG ratio divides the PE ratio by the earnings growth rate, which allows companies with different growth rates to be compared.

The Slater PEG ratio is the forecast rolling PE ratio divided by forecast earnings growth. In addition, the Slater PEG is only quoted when there has been four consecutive years of earnings growth. The lower a company's PEG ratio, the cheaper the company – all other things being equal. A growth company with a current PEG that is below 1 is viewed as good value, while a PEG below 0.75 is viewed as cheap. The screen selects undervalued companies with a Slater PEG of 0.75 or lower.

Rolling PE is less than 20

Companies with a high rolling PE above 20 would need to have earnings growth above 20% to justify such a high valuation. This sort of growth level is not sustainable long term and the share price is likely to be very sensitive to adverse news. For these reasons, expensive companies with a PE ratio above 20 are excluded.

Rolling earnings growing faster than 15%

One of the key contributing factors to stock price appreciation is the future rate of earnings growth. The higher the future earnings growth, the more rapid the price appreciation is likely to be. However, forecast earnings growth tends to be too optimistic at times. It is therefore useful to blend current earnings growth with next year's forecast earnings growth. The rolling one-year earnings growth weights the current year and next year's earnings growth depending on how far a company is through its fiscal year.

Growth companies should have high earnings growth. The screen therefore requires that companies have a one-year rolling earnings growth above 15%.

Relative share price strength over the past year is better than the market

Growth companies are growing their earnings at a faster pace than the average company in the market. This means that the share price of growth companies should be increasing at a faster rate than the price index of the market. That is, they should have positive relative (price) strength when compared to the market. This is especially true when you are selecting cheap growth companies, as they eventually benefit from an upward revaluation, which provides a tailwind to the price. The screen therefore eliminates companies that have underperformed the market.

Return on capital employed is greater than 12%

Return on capital employed (ROCE) compares earnings to the capital used to generate them. ROCE is defined as earnings before interest and tax (EBIT) divided by the net capital employed (NCE). EBIT is pre-tax profit minus net interest earned. Net capital employed is the capital available for use in the business by shareholders, long-term borrowings, company profits or revaluation. It is defined as total assets minus current liabilities.

ROCE measures the return generated by a company on the capital available. In general, a good company should have a high return on capital. A company with ROCE in high double digits is likely to have a competitive edge versus its competitors. The screen looks for companies with a ROCE above 12%.

Market value above £20m – illiquid companies ruled out

The screen removes companies with a market value below £20m. These companies tend to be hard to trade and are riskier. These companies are therefore avoided.

Market value below £1bn – small growth companies

The aim of the Zulu screen is to identify small growth companies, as these have greater scope to grow than larger companies. It is much easier to double a company's profits from £10m to £20m, than a large company's earnings from £1bn to £2bn, as the absolute increase required is smaller (£10m compared to £1bn).

A small growth company will also have a smaller share of the overall market, offering greater scope for organic growth. Companies with a market value below £1bn are defined as small, so those with a market valuation above £1bn are not considered.

Screen 6: Naked growth

The naked growth screen is broadly based on criteria proposed in the book, *The Naked Trader: How Anyone Can Make Money Trading Shares* by Robbie Burns. The aim of the screen is to find excellent companies with good fundamentals that are growing sales, earnings and dividends.

The criteria for the naked growth screen are as follows:

Market value above £20m – illiquid companies ruled out

The screen removes companies with a market value below £20m. These companies tend to be riskier and harder (and more expensive) to trade – most investors do not want to own them. These companies are therefore avoided.

Market value below £1bn – small growth companies

Small companies have greater scope to grow than larger companies. The screen therefore removes companies with a market valuation above £1bn.

Positive sales, earnings and dividend growth

A healthy growth company should be growing sales and earnings each year. Selected companies are therefore required to have rising sales and earnings over the past 12 months.

Growing companies that pay out a dividend must show greater financial discipline and manage cash flow more carefully, which often proves beneficial to the bottom line over the long term. In addition, companies that manage to grow the dividend in line with earnings send a signal that they are intent on progressively rewarding shareholders as growth is achieved. Companies are therefore required to have rising dividends.

Positive share price momentum

Growth companies that are reasonably priced should be steadily rising in value as sales and earnings growth gradually pushes up market value. The screen therefore requires that the current price is higher than the price 52 weeks ago.

More than 5% above 52-week price low

Fairly valued or cheap companies that are expected to continue growing in the future should be gradually increasing in value and prices should not be close to their 52-week lows. If a company's share price is within 5% of its 52-week price low there is a risk that something fundamental has changed and that the growth story is unlikely to continue. The screen avoids companies that are making new lows or are close to making new lows.

Trading spreads are not too wide

If the trading spread (i.e., the difference between the price you can buy and sell at) is more than 4% there are not enough company shares to make the market for company shares liquid. Consequently, the cost of buying and selling the shares is high and it could be difficult to sell shares owned. The screen therefore excludes illiquid companies with spreads of 4% or more.

Rolling PE is less than 20

Companies with a high rolling PE above 20 would need to have earnings growth above 20% to justify such a high valuation (so that the PEG is less than one). This sort of growth level is not sustainable long term and the share price is likely to be very sensitive to adverse news. For these reasons, companies with a PE ratio above 20 are excluded.

A PE ratio above 12 is generally preferred, as this excludes companies that are potential value traps.

Low net debt compared to operating profits

Prudent use of debt increases the financial resources available to a company for growth and expansion. Conversely, a company with a high level of debt may find its freedom of action restricted by creditors or find that high interest-rate costs are starting to hurt profitability. Companies with low levels of debt are therefore preferred.

Debt is judged to be too high for a company if its net debt (which is total debt minus cash equivalents) could not be completely paid off within three years from its full-year operating profits. The screen excludes companies with high debt levels.

Exclude companies that are collective investments

The focus is on finding excellent companies rather than funds. Collective investments are therefore excluded from the screen.

Price to pre-tax profits ratio is less than 15

Price to pre-tax earnings per share (PPTE) ratio, is defined as the company's market value divided by its pre-tax earnings (also referred to as pre-tax profit). Pre-tax profit is operating profit minus interest and any other non-operating expenses (except taxes).

Using this ratio as a measure of valuation is useful as it eliminates the distortion from different corporate tax structures on earnings. (It doesn't eliminate the impact of capital structure though. This ratio could be replaced with price to enterprise value, which accounts for market value and debt levels. However, as enterprise value is evaluated in more detail in later chapters, this won't make too much difference.) Companies that have a market value above 15 times pre-tax profits are judged to be expensive and are excluded by the screen.

Exclude companies listed on AIM

Companies that have a full listing are preferred as the accounting numbers are better audited and are generally more reliable than companies listed on AIM.

Piotroski F-score above 5

The screen requires the Piotroski F-score to be higher than 5, which signals that the financial strength of the company is improving.

Economic moat screen

Companies with an economic moat have a durable competitive advantage that helps protect them from competition and market pressures, just as the moat around a castle protects the castle from invaders. These competitive advantages provide pricing power or cost reductions, which allow these companies to maintain high returns on capital, leading to higher cash flows and returns for investors. The economic moats screen aims to find companies with durable competitive advantages using key metrics that often signal a company has an economic moat.

Income, value or growth companies that are judged to have an economic moat are of interest for investors and should be prioritised over other companies to research and invest in.

The criteria for the economic moat growth screen are as follows:

High free cash flow as a percentage of sales relative to the market

One signal that a company has a durable competitive advantage is the ability to generate a high rate of free cash flow. This is cash generated by the business after all capital expenditures (e.g., factory improvements, machinery repairs and replacement, etc.) have been paid off.

Free cash is cash that can be reinvested by the firm to grow their business, or paid out in dividends. The higher the rate of cash flow generation, the higher the value of the company. Companies with an economic moat are required to have free cash flow to sales in the top 20% of the market.

High operating profit margins above 20% and better than 80% of the market

The operating (profit) margin is a measure of a company's pricing strategy and operating efficiency. The operating margin is defined as operating profit (i.e., profits earned from the company's core business operations) divided by revenue. It measures the proportion of a company's revenue left after paying for variable costs, such as wages or raw materials.

The operating margin is therefore an indicator of how effective the company is at converting revenue into operating profits. Operating margins are generally higher for companies with a competitive advantage as they have greater pricing power and/or cost advantages.

Companies with a strong competitive advantage should have the highest operating margins at above 20%. Consequently, only the top 20% of companies with the highest operating margins in the market are considered, with a 20% hurdle rate for the operating margin.

High returns on capital employed

Companies with a strong, durable competitive advantage can generate high sustainable returns on capital employed (ROCE) and returns on equity (ROE) compared with their peer group. Companies with returns of 15% or higher on a long-term basis may indicate a company with pricing power or cost advantages. Economic moat companies are therefore required to have averaged above 15% returns over the past five years and current returns should also be above 15%.

Companies fully listed on main stock exchange

This screen relies on accounting numbers to indicate whether a competitive advantage exists. These numbers therefore need to be reliable and fully audited. The screen therefore restricts the search to the larger fully listed companies. In the case of the UK, the search is restricted to companies listed on the FTSE 350. For the US, this could be changed to the S&P 500 index.

Summary

Screening for companies is a good place to start your research as it can save time and narrow your focus to a more manageable group of companies. The screens have been designed to select four sub-classes of company: income, value, growth and economic moat.

Income companies generate a sustainable, above-market average income, which can be invested in using tax wrappers, such as ISAs, which lower the tax on dividend income generated. (We discuss how to take advantage of tax rules in chapter 15.)

Value and growth companies aim for capital appreciation, which are suitable for investing outside of tax wrappers and allow you take advantage of capital gains tax allowances. However, our choice of value screen, which insists on some income generation, allows value companies to also sit within tax wrappers as well.

The economic moat screen is designed to provide a list of companies with a competitive advantage. Any companies that appear to overlap with other screens should be prioritised. In addition, cheap companies with an economic moat may be worth analysing, even if they don't register on the other screens.

While share screeners are useful tools, they do have limitations. Share screeners only examine a limited number of quantitative factors – they are not exhaustive (otherwise you would quickly rule out all companies, defeating the purpose of screening for shares in the first place).

Furthermore, screens ignore important qualitative factors, such as the effectiveness of management, the drivers of competitive advantage or whether there are adverse, disruptive factors that are likely to hurt future profits, i.e., pending lawsuits, labour problems or low customer-satisfaction levels.

There are still many other quantitative and qualitative factors to keep in mind when considering whether a company is a worthwhile investment. The following chapters present additional fundamental and qualitative checks that help select the best quality companies with high return potential.

CHAPTER 3

EARNINGS CHECKS

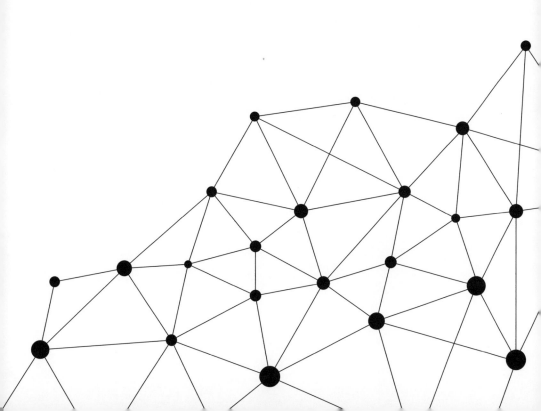

Introduction

F UNDAMENTAL ANALYSIS, WHICH makes use of accounting numbers, allows the best quality companies to be selected from our screened lists of income, value and growth companies. The first set of checks involves looking at historic and forecast earnings.

Earnings information

Earnings information is available on the Morningstar website, which conveniently lists the normalised and reported earnings per share (EPS) over the past ten years. EPS is net income divided by the number of shares outstanding. Reported EPS uses reported earnings in the nominator of the calculation, while normalised EPS uses normalised earnings in the nominator. Normalised earnings exclude anything that is an unusual one-time event, making it easier to identify earnings from core operations.

These figures can be found by entering the company name into the search box at the top of the Morningstar home page. A list of companies that match your search will appear. Selecting a company name will bring up the overview section of the company profile. Both normalised and reported EPS figures for the past ten years can be found on the income statement in the financial section of the company profile.

Paid for data providers (such as Stockopedia, ShareScope and Zacks) also provide consensus broker earnings forecasts for normalised EPS and net profit over the next two years.

Positive earnings

The first thing to assess is whether the company can consistently make a profit. Looking at a company's earnings history will reveal this. Remove any shortlisted companies that have reported a negative normalised or reported EPS figure in the past five years. The preferred trend is for earnings to be positive and steadily rising over the past ten years.

The earnings score counts the number of years where reported and normalised EPS have been positive over the past ten years. Our preference is to invest in companies with a high earnings score of 16 or higher, as these companies are more likely to be consistently profitable.

Example

Table 3.1 shows the earnings history for XP Power, which was selected as an income company. The net profit (also referred to as net earnings or net income) has been positive over the past ten years, indicating that the company is able to consistently make a profit.

Net profit rose until 2011 (ignoring the blip in 2009 because of the financial crisis). Earnings fell in 2012 due to temporary weakness in global demand and then gradually recover. Net profits in 2017 are 3.2 times those in 2008.

Similarly, reported and normalised EPS were positive for each of the past ten years. The earnings score is therefore 20. The normalised earnings trend has been volatile, but the underlying trend is upward.

Table 3.1 Earnings per share (EPS) history – XP Power

	2008	2009	2010	2011	2012	2013	2014	2015	2016	2017
Net Profit (£m)	8.8	7.4	15.8	20.3	15.5	18.2	19.4	19.7	21.3	28.3
Reported EPS (p)	46.5	39.4	83.9	107.1	81.7	95.8	102.1	103.7	112.0	148.3
Normalised EPS (p)	46.4	39.3	83.2	106.4	81.3	95.1	101.1	102.8	111.2	146.0

Earnings growth

Earnings growth is the annual rate of growth of earnings. This measure ensures that the company becomes more valuable over time and that the share price will eventually appreciate. In addition, for income companies, an increase in earnings ensures that dividends will continue to be paid and that there is greater scope to increase dividends paid out in the future.

Normalised earnings are used to assess earnings growth as this measure excludes exceptional items. Growth companies should have strong earnings growth, at more than 15% per annum over the past five years – anything less and the company is not growing fast enough and should be removed from the shortlist.

For income and value companies you want to select companies that have sustainable earnings growth, with earnings growing between 3% and 15% per annum over the past five years. This makes it more likely that dividends and/or value will be grown over time.

Remove shortlisted companies, whose normalised earnings growth is less than 3% over five years, as you want companies that increase earnings faster than long-term inflation. Equally, companies that are growing over 15% per annum are in a growth phase, which may not be sustainable. If five-year earnings growth is in excess of 15% per annum look at earnings growth over ten years (or the longest history available) and ensure this is also in excess of 5%.

Example

Normalised earnings growth for XP Power is summarised in table 3.2. Looking at table 3.1, the five-year compound annual growth rate (CAGR) for normalised earnings is 12.4% (= $(146.0 \div 81.3)^{(1/5)}$ - 1). This is higher than our cut-off point of 3% growth and the CAGR of earnings from 2008 to 2017 was 13.6% (= $(146.0 \div 46.4)^{(1/9)}$ - 1). Note XP Power had strong earnings growth in 2017 due to a sharp global upturn in trading conditions, which boosted earnings by more than 30%.

Table 3.2 Annualised EPS growth – XP Power

	Annualised EPS Growth (%)
1 Year	31.3
3 Years	13.0
5 Years	12.4
9 Years	13.6

Broker views – Future expected earnings growth

If broker forecasts for future EPS growth over the next two years are positive, it indicates that the market expects the company's profits to grow over the near term.

For income or value companies, check that the consensus forecasts are higher than the latest EPS available. Ideally, prospective EPS growth should be more than inflation (3%) and preferably above 5%, but it is not a prerequisite. A company with low earnings growth is factored in when estimating the underlying broker value of the company. (Broker valuations are discussed in chapter 11.)

Example

Broker forecasts of earnings growth for XP Power are shown in table 3.3. Broker consensus expect earnings to grow by 20.6% in 2018 and by 7.7% in 2019. Earnings growth is therefore expected to be comfortably above the 3% hurdle.

Table 3.3 Broker forecasts – Earnings growth for XP Power

	2017	2018 (f)	2019 (f)
Normalised EPS (p)	146.0	176.0	189.5
Earnings Growth (%)	31.3	20.6	7.7

(f) indicates broker forecasts, taken at December 2018

For growth companies, consensus broker forecasts should expect growth to continue. If brokers don't anticipate decent earnings growth, there may be a problem with the investment thesis for continued growth.

Consensus broker forecasts should suggest prospective EPS growth above 10% per annum over the next two years. Remove growth companies from the shortlist that are not growing normalised earnings fast enough. In addition, remove companies if their EPS has not risen over the latest four years of numbers available (including the two years of broker forecasts).

Example

Table 3.4 shows the consensus broker forecasts for growth company Bloomsbury Publishing. Normalised EPS has increased each year since 2014, except for 2017. This fall in earnings in 2017 is attributable to increased investment in the development of new digital content to support future growth and the ending of a contract with the Qatar Foundation.

Broker consensus expects earnings to grow by 18.2% in 2019 and 13.3% in 2020. This equates to earnings growth of 15.7% per annum over the next two years, well above the 10% growth hurdle. EPS is expected to reach a new high of 16.2p by 2020, which implies earnings are expected to grow relative to the 2016 level.

Table 3.4 Broker forecasts – Earnings growth for Bloomsbury Publishing

	2014	2015	2016	2017	2018	2019 (f)	2020 (f)
Normalised EPS (p)	11.3	12.7	14.0	10.8	12.1	14.3	16.2
Earnings Growth (%)		12.4	10.2	-22.9	12.0	18.2	13.3

(f) indicates broker forecasts, taken at December 2018.

Stockopedia provides a summary of how much broker forecasts have changed over the past month and three months. Upward revisions in earnings are desirable as they indicate that market sentiment has turned more positive on the earnings potential of the company, which is supportive of upward price momentum. Conversely, downward revisions may reflect the market turning more negative on the earnings potential of a company, which may lead to some price weakness.

Example

Table 3.5 shows the change in broker earnings forecasts for XP Power in 2018 and 2019 in December 2018. Earnings forecasts are positive for 2018 but negative for 2019, indicating that market consensus has turned less positive on the company's earning potential for 2019.

Table 3.5 – Detailed broker forecasts – XP Power

	31st December 2018			31st December 2019		
	Net Profit (£m)	DPS (p)	EPS (p)	Net Profit (£m)	DPS (p)	EPS (p)
Consensus	32.4	82.4	176.0	36.3	87.5	189.5
1m Change	0.0%	0.0%	0.0%	0.0%	0.0%	0.0%
3m Change	-2.0%	1.2%	0.1%	-2.2%	-0.4%	-3.6%

Pre-tax profits

Pre-tax profits exclude the effects of tax, which vary from year to year due to different tax allowances. Declining pre-tax profits (or declining pre-tax profit margins) can quickly translate into declining EPS and a falling share price. We therefore require that pre-tax profit grows by more than 3% per annum over the past five years for income or value companies, or more than 15% for growth companies. Broker forecasts for pre-tax profit growth should be in line with prospective EPS growth. Companies should be removed from the shortlist if pre-tax profits are not growing sufficiently.

Example

Table 3.6 shows the available history of pre-tax profits for XP Power. Pretax profits have not risen every year, but the underlying trend is upward.

Pre-tax profits rose from £20.2m in 2012 to £32.2m in 2017. This equates to a 9.8% (= $(32.2 \div 20.2)^{(1/5)} - 1$) rise over the past five years. Pre-tax profits are expected to rise by 23.2% (= $39.7 \div 32.2 - 1$) in 2018 and by 11.3% (= $44.2 \div 39.7 - 1$) in 2019. Pre-tax profit growth is therefore expected to be above the 3% hurdle.

Table 3.6 Pre-tax profit – XP Power

	2010	2011	2012	2013	2014	2015	2016	2017	2018 (f)	2019 (f)
Pre-Tax Profit (£m)	18.6	24.3	20.2	22.9	24.3	25.4	27.8	32.2	39.7	44.2

(f) indicates broker forecasts, taken at December 2018.

In general, you should look for companies that are not valued at more than 15 times current pre-tax profits. Companies that have a market value above 15 times current pre-tax profits are viewed as expensive and are removed from the shortlist.

Example

The market capitalisation of XP Power mid-December 2018 was £434.7m. This market value is 13.5 (= 434.7 ÷ 32.2) times 2017 pre-tax profits. Broker consensus is that this multiple will fall to 10.9 times in 2018 and to 9.8 times in 2019. Market value is less than 15 times current pre-tax profits and, based on this metric, XP Power is not viewed as expensive.

Pre-tax profit margins, defined as pre-tax profits divided by revenue from sales, should be stable or gradually rising. A sharp fall in profit margins is a warning sign of further potential trouble ahead. If pre-tax profit margins have fallen sharply in the latest reported year, the company can be removed from the buy list.

Example

Pre-tax profit margins for XP Power are calculated in table 3.7. Pre-tax profit margins have remained reasonably stable, ranging between 19.3% and 24% in 2010–2017. Profit margin for 2017 was weaker than previous years. However, broker consensus expects profit margins to be close to or above 20% in 2018–2019.

Table 3.7 Pre-tax profit margin – XP Power

	2010	2011	2012	2013	2014	2015	2016	2017	2018 (f)	2019 (f)
Norm. Pre-Tax Profit (£m)	18.6	24.3	20.2	22.9	24.3	25.4	27.8	32.2	39.7	44.2
Revenue (£m)	91.8	103.6	93.9	101.1	101.1	109.7	129.8	166.8	199.0	212.8
Pre-Tax Profit Margin (%)	20.3	23.5	21.5	22.7	24.0	23.2	21.4	19.3	19.9	20.7

(f) indicates broker forecasts, taken at December 2018

Earnings valuation

The prospective PE ratio (also referred to as the forward PE ratio) is price divided by the consensus forecast for EPS over the next 12 months. For income or value companies, a prospective PE ratio of 20 or more is considered expensive and is removed from the shortlist. Companies with a PE ratio below 5 are removed from the watch list, as PE ratios below this level are generally indicative of severe problems or concerns over the long-term viability of the company.

Example

The share price of XP Power was 2130p towards the end of December 2018. Using the normalised EPS figures in table 3.3, the current and prospective PE ratios can be calculated. These are shown in table 3.8. The current PE ratio is 14.6 (= 2130 ÷ 146). Using this metric, XP Power does not look too expensive. Anticipated EPS growth is expected to lead to an improved valuation over the next two years. The company's PE ratio is expected to fall to 12.1 based on forecast EPS for 2018 and to 11.2 based on forecast EPS for 2019.

Table 3.8 PE ratios – XP Power

Ratio	2017	2018 (f)	2019 (f)
PE Ratio	14.6	12.1	11.2

(f) indicates broker forecasts, taken at December 2018.

In general, for income and value companies a PE ratio in high single digits or low double digits is preferred. However, for growth companies, the prospective PE ratio may be high because earnings are growing rapidly. For growth companies, a prospective PE ratio of 40 or more is considered expensive and is removed from the shortlist.

The prospective price-earnings growth (PEG) rate is an alternative valuation measure that aims to take account of earnings growth. It is defined as prospective price to earnings divided by future earnings growth.

In general, a PEG below 1 is deemed to offer excellent value, while a PEG between 1 and 1.5 offers good value. A PEG between 1.5 and 2 is considered average, while a PEG above 2 is considered poor value.

For large cap companies (such as those listed on the FTSE 100) a prospective PEG of 0.75 or lower is considered to be undervalued, while for mid to small cap companies (such as those listed on the FTSE 250 of FTSE small cap) a prospective PEG of 0.6 or lower is required, to offset the additional associated risks. If the PEG is below 0.3 the valuation is considered 'too good to be true' and the company is removed from the watch list.

Example

PEG ratios for XP Power can be calculated from the PE ratios in table 3.8 and the earnings growth numbers in table 3.3. The current PEG ratio is 0.5 (= 14.6 ÷ 31.3), which implies that the PE ratio is two times earnings growth. The prospective PEG rises to 0.6 (= 12.1 ÷ 20.6) for 2018 and 1.5 (= 11.2 ÷ 7.7) in 2019. This suggests that once earnings growth is factored in, the share price offers average value for 2019. If XP Power was a growth company, you would want to look at other companies in the sector which may offer better value. However, as XP Power is an income company you can put this down as a weakness and consider other checks and analysis when deciding whether to invest.

Table 3.9 PEG ratios – Company ABC

Ratio	2017	2018 (f)	2019 (f)
PEG Ratio	0.5	0.6	1.5

(f) indicates broker forecasts, taken at December 2018.

Summary

This chapter has covered a range of earnings and pre-tax profit checks that start to provide insight into the quality of earnings and value of a company.

Companies on the shortlist should ideally have the following characteristics:

Earnings checks

- Earnings positive and trending upwards over the past ten years.
- Normalised EPS numbers over the past five years are positive.
- Five-year average earnings growth is 15% or more for growth companies.
- Five-year average earnings growth is between 3% and 15% for income and value companies.
- Prospective earnings growth should be positive for income or value companies and more than 10% for growth companies.

Pre-tax profits checks

- For value or income companies, pre-tax profit should be growing by more than 3% per annum over the past five years.

- Pre-tax profit for growth companies should be growing by more than 15% per annum over the past five years.

- Broker forecasts for pre-tax profit growth should be in line with prospective EPS growth.

- Market capitalisation less than 15 times pre-tax profits.

- Pre-tax margins are stable or gradually rising.

Earnings valuations

- Current and prospective PE ratios between 5 and 20 for income and value companies.

- PEG ratio less than 0.75 for large growth companies, or less than 0.6 for small and medium growth companies.

CHAPTER 4

SALES CHECKS

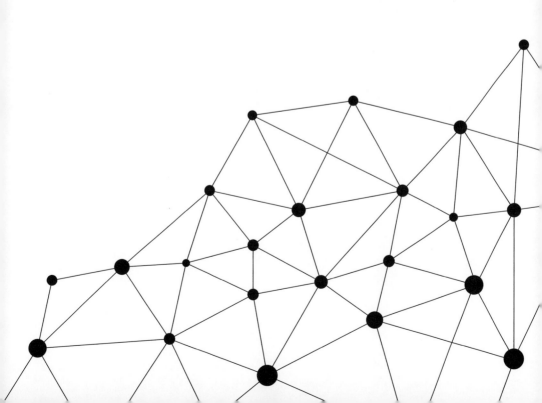

Introduction

S ALES (OR REVENUE) refers to the money received by a company from the sale of goods and services. Sales trends are an important measure of a company's long-term performance and prospects, as achieving greater profitability over the long term requires growing revenues.

Sales information

Sales information for the past ten years is available on the Morningstar website. Sales figures for the past ten years can be found on the income statement in the financial section of the company profile. Sales per share (SPS) is sales divided by the number of shares outstanding.

Paid for data providers (such as Stockopedia, ShareScope and Zacks) provide consensus broker sales forecasts over the next two years.

Sales growth

Sales growth should be stable or trending upwards, signalling an expanding market for the company's products or services. If sales are trending down, future rises in earnings are unlikely to continue unless sales growth resumes. Remove companies from the shortlist that have not grown their sales over the past five years. The only exception is if the company has a large market capitalisation (in excess of several billion pounds) and has already experienced a significant fall in price; it may then be worth looking at the company as a recovery play.

Example

Sales growth for XP Power is summarised in table 4.1. The five-year compound annual growth rate (CAGR) for sales is 12.2% (= $(166.8 \div 93.9)^{(1/5)} - 1$). XP Power has therefore managed to expand the market for its products, or charge more for those products, over the past five years. The CAGR of sales from 2010 to 2017 is 8.9% (= $(166.8 \div 91.8)^{(1/7)} - 1$). Sales growth has accelerated over the last few years with three-year growth of 18.2% and one-year growth of 28.5%. Broker consensus is that sales growth will slow to 19.3% in 2018 and 6.9% in 2019.

Table 4.1 Annualised sales growth – XP Power

	2010	2011	2012	2013	2014	2015	2016	2017	2018 (f)	2019 (f)
Sales (£m)	91.8	103.6	93.9	101.1	101.1	109.7	129.8	166.8	199.0	212.8

	Annualised Sales Growth (%)
1 Year	28.5
3 Year	18.2
5 Year	12.2
7 Year	8.9
2018 (f)	19.3
2019 (f)	6.9

(f) indicates broker forecasts, taken at December 2018.

Sales valuation

The price to sales ratio (PSR) for a company is calculated by dividing the company's market capitalisation by its sales in the most recent year; or, equivalently, the share price divided by sales per share. It reflects the value placed on sales by the market. A lower value indicates that the company is less popular and potentially better value.

However, it should be noted that the PSR is sensitive to sector differences. For example, companies with high profit margins and strong growth (such as technology companies) typically have high PSRs, while companies with high turnover and low profit margins (such as supermarkets) typically have low PSRs.

In general, a useful guide is that a company with a PSR over 5 is deemed to be expensive, while a PSR below 3 is likely to be good value. A PSR below 1 may offer excellent value. However, companies with PSRs approaching or below 0.1 may be 'too good to be true' and should be avoided. Similarly, companies with PSRs above 20 are thought of as very expensive and should be avoided.

Looking at the highest and lowest PSR figures over the past five years helps to give an indication of where future PSRs (and hence prices) might lie. Ideally the current PSR should be below the average company PSR for the last five years. Eliminate companies from the shortlist if the current PSR is above the average of the highest PSRs over the past five years.

It is worth looking at the sector and market average PSRs. This gives an indication of whether the company is undervalued or not against its peer group. If the company PSR is more than 1.5 times the sector average PSR remove it from consideration.

Example

To calculate the PSRs you will need to calculate the sales per share, as Morningstar doesn't provide this on their company pages or stock profile. Sales per share is sales revenue divided by the total number of shares outstanding. Sales information for XP Power is in table 4.1. While Morningstar doesn't explicitly state the number of shares outstanding, it can be proxied by dividing the profit for the tax year by reported EPS and multiplying by 100. Alternatively, Stockopedia has up to five years of numbers on its company pages.

To estimate the number of shares outstanding in forecast years you can either use the current number of shares (if the number of outstanding shares has been gradually decreasing) or you can assume that the number of shares outstanding grows at a similar pace to recent history. The CAGR in shares outstanding is 1.0% (= 19.4 ÷ 19.2 − 1). The number of outstanding shares is therefore estimated to be 19.6m (= 19.4m × (1 + 1.0%)) in 2018 and 19.8m (= 19.6m × (1 + 1.0%)) in 2019. Sales per share can then be calculated.

Table 4.2 Sales per share calculation – XP Power

	2010	2011	2012	2013	2014	2015	2016	2017	2018 (f)	2019 (f)
Sales (£m)	91.8	103.6	93.9	101.1	101.1	109.7	129.8	166.8	199.0	212.8
Shares Outstanding (m)	19.0	19.1	19.1	19.1	19.2	19.2	19.2	19.4	19.6	19.8
Sales per Share (SPS) (p)	483.2	542.9	492.8	528.0	526.7	572.2	677.4	860.3	1014.4	1072.1

(f) indicates broker forecasts, taken at December 2018.

Table 4.3 shows the calculation of the PSR ranges for XP Power. The highest and lowest price the company's shares traded at in each year are shown in the first two rows. The low price to sales ratio for a given year is calculated by dividing the low price by sales per share (SPS) in the same year. Similarly, the highest price sales ratio is calculated by dividing the high price by sales per share (SPS) in the same year.

Table 4.3 PSR ranges – XP Power

	2013	2014	2015	2016	2017	Average
High Price (p)	1630.0	1798.0	1750.0	1845.1	3626.4	
Low Price (p)	972.3	1340.0	1375.0	1396.8	1725.0	
Sales per Share (SPS) (p)	528.0	526.7	572.2	677.4	860.3	
PSR low	1.8	2.5	2.4	2.1	2.0	2.2
PSR high	3.1	3.4	3.1	2.7	4.2	3.3

XP Power's PSR has ranged from 1.8 to 4.2 over the past five years. The average low PSR is 2.2 (= (1.8 + 2.5 + 2.4 + 2.1 + 2.0) ÷ 5) and the average high PSR is 3.3. If the current PSR is below 2.2 the PSR is starting to offer good value, while a PSR above 3.3 is poor value.

Table 4.4 PSRs – XP Power

	2017	2018 (f)	2019 (f)
Price to Sales Ratio (PSR)	2.5	2.1	2.0

(f) indicates broker forecasts, taken at December 2018.

Table 4.4 shows the current and prospective PSRs, when the current price for XP Power is 2130p. The current PSR is 2.5 (= 2130 ÷ 860.3). The PSR is expected to fall to 2.1 (= 2130 ÷ 1014.4) in 2018 and 2.0 (= 2130 ÷ 1072.1) in 2019. This suggests that the shares offer average to good value based on the past range (and good value based on the general guidelines).

Inventory to sales ratio

The inventory to sales ratio is average inventory divided by sales. Looking at this ratio over time provides an indication of how inventory is being managed, since it can signal potential problems with cash flow and profitability.

Ideally the current inventory to sales ratio should be stable or falling. The latter indicates that inventory is shrinking (because it is being sold) or that sales are growing more rapidly than inventory. An increase in the inventory to sales ratio signals that either inventory is growing faster than sales or sales are dropping. A sharp increase in the ratio is often a signal of problems ahead.

Example

Table 4.5 shows the calculation for the inventory to sales ratio. The ratio has remained stable over the past decade, so inventory has grown in line with sales and there is currently no immediate concern.

Table 4.5 Inventory to sales ratio – XP Power

	2008	2009	2010	2011	2012	2013	2014	2015	2016	2017
Inventory (£m)	17.5	10.7	21.0	22.0	19.8	20.4	25.2	28.7	32.2	37.8
Average Inventory (£m)		14.1	15.9	21.5	20.9	20.1	22.8	27.0	30.5	35.0
Sales (£m)		67.3	91.8	103.6	93.9	101.1	101.1	109.7	129.8	166.8
Inventory to Sales Ratio (ISR)		0.2	0.2	0.2	0.2	0.2	0.2	0.2	0.2	0.2

Receivables to sales ratio

The receivables to sales ratio is average accounts receivable divided by total sales. This ratio gives the proportion of sales that are unpaid. If this ratio is high and approaching 1, it means that a significant amount of cash is tied up with slow-paying customers. A high ratio may also be a sign of aggressive or fraudulent booking of revenue, when little of the sales will be converted to cash and sales will be logged as high levels of accounts receivable instead, pushing the ratio up. You therefore want to avoid investing in companies with ratios above 0.70. The ideal situation is for the receivables to sales ratio to be low and for the historic trend to be stable or trending down.

Example

The calculation of the receivables to sales ratio (RSR) for XP Power is shown in table 4.6. The historic RSR is low and has been stable over the past. There are no red flags here.

Table 4.6 Receivables to sales ratio – XP Power

	2008	2009	2010	2011	2012	2013	2014	2015	2016	2017
Accounts Receivable (£m)	12.1	11.0	19.5	20.2	16.6	16.4	16.9	18.2	22.2	27.0
Average Account Receivable (£m)		11.6	15.3	19.9	18.4	16.5	16.7	17.6	20.2	24.6
Sales (£m)		67.3	91.8	103.6	93.9	101.1	101.1	109.7	129.8	166.8
Receivables to Sales Ratio (RSR)		0.2	0.2	0.2	0.2	0.2	0.2	0.2	0.2	0.1

Summary

This chapter has covered a range of sales checks that start to provide insight into the performance prospects of a company. Companies on the shortlist should ideally have the following characteristics:

Revenue checks

• Sales growth is positive and is expected to continue.

• The inventory to sales ratio is stable or falling.

• The receivables to sales ratio is low and stable or declining.

Sales valuation

• The PSR is less than 5, although less than 3 is preferred.

• The company PSR is less than 1.5 times the sector PSR.

CHAPTER 5

CASH-FLOW CHECKS

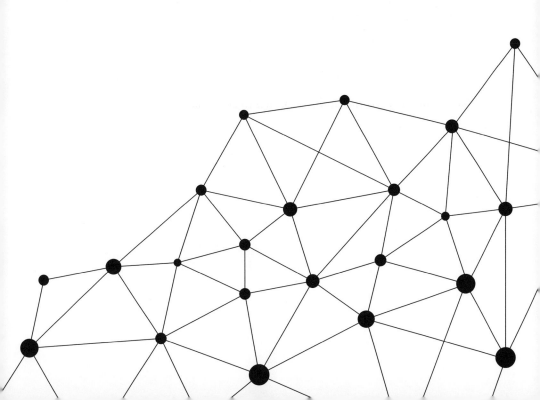

Introduction

C ASH FLOW IS the movement of money into or out of a company from operating, investing and financing activities. Cash is of vital importance to the health of a company. Without positive cash flow a company will eventually be unable to meet its financial obligations, thereby leading to a cash crunch or bankruptcy. Cash-flow checks help provide valuable information on a company's quality of earnings, their liquidity or solvency, and their financial situation.

Quality of earnings cash indicator

A company has high-quality earnings if the stated earnings are a true representation of what the company is generating in terms of cash earnings. Unfortunately, not all companies have high-quality earnings.

While reported earnings may be within the law, according to Generally Accepted Accounting Principles (GAAP), there is plenty of scope to inaccurately reflect the cash earnings of a company. Sometimes the requirements of the accounting principles may be to blame for this discrepancy; other times it may be due to choices made by management. In either case, reported figures that do not portray the real cash earnings of the company can mislead investors into making bad investment decisions.

The best way to evaluate quality of earnings for a company is to compare cash flow per share to the reported and normalised EPS figures. Investors can rely on cash flow as it is harder to manipulate than net earnings (although it can still be done to a certain degree).

Cash flow per share (CFPS) is available in the cash flow statement in the financial section of the company profile on the Morningstar website.

If operating cash flow per share (that is, operating cash flow divided by the number of shares outstanding) is greater than reported EPS, earnings are of high quality because the company is generating more cash than is reported on the income statement. Conversely, if operating cash flow per share is less than reported EPS, the company is generating less cash than is being reported on the income statement. In this case, EPS is of low quality because it does not reflect the negative operating results of the company and overstates the true (cash) operating results.

CFPS is required to be greater than EPS in the latest accounting year. Ideally, the ratio of CFPS to EPS should be higher than 1.5. Companies not meeting this criterion are removed from our shortlist. You should also check that the five-year average of CFPS is in excess of average EPS over the last five years. Again, companies that do not meet this requirement are removed from the shortlist.

Example

Table 5.1 shows the operating CFPS and EPS history for XP Power. CFPS in 2017 was 152.2p, which is above the normalised EPS of 146p. However, the ratio of CFPS to EPS in 2014 is only 1.04 (= 152.2 ÷ 146.0). It is notable that CFPS was below EPS in 2010 and 2011, raising concerns over the quality of earnings. The average CFPS over the past five years is 124.5p, compared with an average EPS of 111.2p. This gives a CFPS to EPS ratio of 1.1 (= 124.5 ÷ 111.2).

While earnings are covered by operating cash flow over the past five years, the quality of earnings could be higher. The CFPS to EPS ratio is not low enough to remove XP Power from consideration; however, it should be noted as a weak area. Other cash-flow metrics should be considered before deciding whether to invest.

Table 5.1 Cash flow and earnings per share – XP Power

	2008	2009	2010	2011	2012	2013	2014	2015	2016	2017
Reported EPS (p)	46.5	39.4	83.9	107.1	81.7	95.8	102.1	103.7	112.0	148.3
Normalised EPS (p)	46.4	39.3	83.2	106.4	81.3	95.1	101.1	102.8	111.2	146.0
Cash Flow per Share (CFPS) (p)	36.4	80.6	49.5	79.6	121.2	103.9	113.1	109.0	144.6	152.2

Cash to capital expenditure

Cash from operating activities is important because all company expenses ultimately need to be paid with cash generated from activities. Surplus cash flow can be used to expand business operations and boost future earnings, which will eventually drive the share price higher and allow for increased dividend payments.

Capital expenditure per share (capex ps) is the amount per share the company invests in the business to acquire or upgrade physical assets, such as buildings and equipment. You want to avoid companies that have high capital expenditure relative to operating cash flow, as it limits the company's ability to grow future earnings.

Capex ps is available under ratios in the financial section of the company profile on Morningstar.

As capital expenditure is cyclical, average capital expenditure per share over the past five years is compared to the average cash flow per share over the past five years. If average capital expenditure is more than average cash flow, the company does not consistently generate excess cash and should be removed from the shortlist. In general, you should prefer companies that have comparatively low levels of capital expenditure relative to operating cash flow.

Surplus cash flow for a company is defined as CFPS minus capital expenditure per share and dividend per share. Ideally, surplus cash flow should be positive and more than 20% of the operating cash flow per share.

Example

Table 5.2 shows the information required to calculate surplus cash flow. Cash flow is well above capital expenditure over the past five years. This means that it has been able to generate free cash flow (which is cash flow minus capital expenditure) every year. CFPS averaged 124.5p over the past five years, while capital expenditure per share was 32.5p. This means that on average 26.1% (= 32.5 ÷ 124.5) of operating cash flow goes on capital expenditure.

Surplus cash flow per share has been positive over the past five years, indicating that there is cash left over after capital expenditure and dividends have been paid for. Surplus cash flow per share averaged 32.4p compared with 124.5p of operating CFPS. This means that on average 26.0% (= 32.4 ÷ 124.5) of operating cash flow is surplus cash, which is above the required 20% threshold. However, it is worth noting surplus cash flow dropped to 14.5% in 2017.

Table 5.2 Cash flow, capital expenditure and dividend per share history – XP Power

	2013	2014	2015	2016	2017	Average
Cash Flow per Share (CFPS) (p)	103.9	113.1	109.0	144.6	152.2	124.5
Capex per Share (Capex ps) (p)	16.7	30.2	28.2	35.5	52.1	32.5
Dividend per Share (DPS) (p)	45.1	50.0	54.1	71.0	78.0	59.6
Free Cash Flow per Share (FCFPS) (p)	87.2	82.8	80.8	109.1	100.1	92.0
Surplus Cash Flow per Share (SCFPS) (p)	42.1	32.8	26.7	38.1	22.1	32.4
SCFPS ÷ CFPS (%)	40.5	29.0	24.5	26.3	14.5	26.0

Cash valuation

The price to cash flow (PCF) ratio is used to compare a company's market value to its cash flow. It is calculated by dividing share price by CFPS from the latest accounts. In theory, the lower a company's PCF ratio, the better value the company. Morningstar states the current company PCF in the overview section of the company profile.

As a general guide, companies with a PCF ratio below 15 offer good value, while companies with a PCF between 5 and 10 may offer excellent value. Companies with PCF ratios below 5 are treated as 'too good to be true' and may well be in trouble. Companies with PCF ratios above 20 are poor value, and ratios above 40 are very expensive and should be avoided.

For income and value companies, the preference is for the PCF ratio to lie between 5 and 15. Companies with a ratio above 20 are removed from the shortlist. Growth companies may have higher ratios, as cash is growing rapidly, but you should remove growth companies from the shortlist when the ratio is above 40.

Example

Table 5.3 shows the current PCF ratio for XP Power. From table 5.2, CFPS in 2017 is 152.2p. Towards the end of December the share price for XP Power was 2130p, giving a PCF ratio of 14.0 (= 2130 ÷ 152.2).

Table 5.3 PCF ratio – XP Power

Ratio	2017
PCF ratio	14.0

Summary

Cash-flow checks can be summarised as follows:

Cash checks

- Operating CFPS is greater than 1.5 times reported EPS in the latest accounting year.

- Average CFPS over five years is 1.5 times the five-year average of reported EPS.

- Average capital expenditure per share over the past five years is consistently less than average CFPS.

- Ideally surplus cash flow should be positive and more than 20% of the operating cash flow.

Cash valuation

- Company PCF ratio is more than 5 and less than 15.

CHAPTER 6

DIVIDEND CHECKS

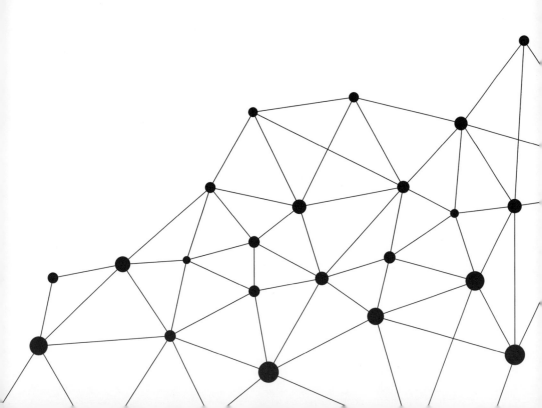

Introduction

IVIDENDS ARE THE sum of money paid regularly by a company to its shareholders out of its profits (or reserves). For income companies, it's important to check that payment of future dividends is sustainable and therefore likely to continue. It is also important to check that the dividends have scope to grow above the rate of inflation over time.

Progressive dividend history

A rising dividend is a signal that an income company is confident in its prospects. You can check that there has been a gradual increase in the dividend by looking at the history of dividends per share (DPS). Morningstar provides a history of DPS in the financial section of the company profile. If the dividend has been cut in the past five years, the company can be removed from consideration.

The dividend growth rate trend should also be considered. A company that has markedly slowed its dividend growth rate or has held the dividend constant for a few years may be signalling trouble ahead. Of course, every company's dividend growth rate will eventually slow as they mature, but the decline will likely be gradual and steady. If there is an abrupt slowdown in the dividend growth rate, there may be trouble ahead for the company.

Example

Table 6.1 shows the dividend history for XP Power. Dividends have been gradually rising since 2010. Over the past five years, dividends have grown by 13.7% per annum (= $(78 \div 41)^{(1/5)} - 1$). However, dividend growth slowed in 2017, albeit growing at a healthy 9.9%.

Table 6.1 Dividend per share – XP Power

	2010	2011	2012	2013	2014	2015	2016	2017	2018 (f)	2019 (f)
Dividend per share (p)	27.1	36.9	41.0	45.1	50.0	54.1	71.0	78.0	82.5	87.5
DPS growth (%)		36.4	11.1	10.0	10.9	8.2	31.2	9.9	5.7	6.1

(f) indicates broker forecasts, taken at December 2018.

Expected future dividends

Consensus broker forecasts for dividends over the next two years can be found on Stockopedia on the main company profile. Ideally, the consensus dividend forecast for the following year should be higher than the previous year; this indicates that the market doesn't anticipate that the dividend will be cut. Eliminate income companies from the shortlist where forecast dividends are cut.

Example

Table 6.1 shows that the broker consensus expects dividends to grow by 5.7% (= 82.5 ÷ 78 – 1) in 2018 (slower than in 2017) and by 6.1% (= 87.5 ÷ 82.5 – 1) in 2019. The growth rate is therefore expected to be slower than previous years. However, a growth rate above 5% is still reasonably good.

Dividend cover

Companies that aren't generating enough profit (or free cash) to cover the dividend are more likely to cut the dividend. Dividend cover is EPS divided by DPS, which indicates how many times the dividend is covered by earnings.

Looking at just one year of data can be misleading as a company could have an unusually good or bad year. One needs to look at the overall trend of historic dividend cover and the projected dividend cover, which is based on broker forecasts of earnings and dividends. If dividend cover is declining, it can be a sign that the dividend payout is becoming riskier and may not be sustained.

Morningstar provides a history of dividend cover in the income statement of the financial section of the company profile. Forecasts for dividend cover over the next two years are stated in the Stockopedia company profile. Ideally the company should have a stable, or gradually increasing, dividend cover that remains above 2. If dividend cover looks like it is trending down and will fall below 1.5, eliminate the company from the shortlist.

Example

XP Power's dividend cover history is shown in table 6.2. The dividend cover has been gradually trending down since 2010. However, broker consensus expects the dividend cover to improve as well as be above 2 in 2018 and 2019.

Table 6.2 Dividend cover – XP Power

	2010	2011	2012	2013	2014	2015	2016	2017	2018 (f)	2019 (f)
Normalised EPS (p)	83.2	106.4	81.3	95.1	101.1	102.8	111.2	146.0	176.0	189.5
Dividend per share (p)	27.1	36.9	41.0	45.1	50.0	54.1	71.0	78.0	82.5	87.5
Dividend Cover	3.1	2.9	2.0	2.1	2.0	1.9	1.6	1.9	2.1	2.2

(f) indicates broker forecasts, taken at December 2018.

Dividend outlook

Dividend statements in annual reports, interim statements and news releases can provide an indication of a company's commitment to maintaining and growing the dividends paid out. You should look for companies that have a positive dividend outlook and a strong commitment to growing the dividend over time.

Read the last few years' dividend statements in the annual and interim reports (usually available on a company's website for investors) to get a better understanding of whether a company has been able to deliver on the dividend growth it anticipated so far. You should also look for guidance on what the company is aiming to pay out in dividends over the next few years.

Example

XP Power has pursued a progressive dividend policy over the past ten years, supported by strong cash flow generation. XP Power's policy expects to continue increasing dividends, while maintaining a dividend cover around 2.

Average future five-year dividend yield

To calculate the average dividend yield over the next five years, a conservative estimate of future dividend growth is needed as well as the latest reported annual dividend and share price.

It is assumed that future dividend growth can be proxied by the minimum growth rate of dividends, earnings and revenue over the past five years. If the earnings or revenue growth rate is below the dividend growth rate, the future dividend growth rate will be restricted.

The next five years of dividends are estimated to be:

$$D_1 = (1 + g) \times D_0$$

$$D_2 = (1 + g) \times D_1$$

$$D_3 = (1 + g) \times D_2$$

$$D_4 = (1 + g) \times D_3$$

$$D_5 = (1 + g) \times D_4$$

This is where D_0 is the latest reported annual dividend, g is future dividend growth and D_i is the dividend paid i years into the future.

Therefore, the average dividend paid out over the next five years can be calculated using $D_{avg} = (D_1 + D_2 + D_3 + D_4 + D_5) \div 5$. The average dividend yield over the next five years is then calculated by dividing this average by the share price, i.e., $D_{avg} \div P$.

Example

From table 6.2, XP Power's dividend was 78p in 2017, meaning that dividends grew by 13.7% over the past five years. Previous chapters have shown that average earnings grew by 12.4% and sales grew by 12.2% per annum. The future dividend growth is therefore assumed to be 12.2%.

This means that the annual DPS over the next five years is expected to be 87.5p (= 78p × 1.122), 98.2p (= 87.5p × 1.122), 110.1p (= 98.2p × 1.122), 123.5p (= 110.1p × 1.122) and 138.6p (= 123.5p × 1.122).

The average dividend over the next five years is D_{avg} = 111.6p (= (87.5p + 98.2p + 110.1p + 123.5p + 138.6p) ÷ 5). The average dividend yield over the next five years is therefore 5.2% (= 111.6p ÷ 2130p).

If you want to be more sophisticated, you can determine the average five-year dividend yield using the broker consensus dividend forecasts to augment the calculation. In this case, the broker's forecasts for year one and two are used for D_1 and D_2, respectively. The remaining three years of future dividends (D_3, D_4, and D_5) are calculated as before.

Example

XP Power's consensus broker forecasts for 2018 and 2019 are 82.5p and 87.5p (from table 6.2). If future dividends then grow by 8.6%, dividends in years three to five will be 98.2p (= 87.5p × 1.122), 110.1p (= 98.2p × 1.122) and 123.5p (= 110.1p × 1.122).

The average dividend over the next five years is D_{avg} = 100.3p (= (82.5p + 87.5p + 98.2p + 110.1p + 123.5p) ÷ 5). The average dividend yield over the next five years is therefore 4.7% (= 100.3p ÷ 2130p).

Income companies are removed from the shortlist if they do not offer an average dividend yield in excess of the market dividend yield plus 1%, with a maximum requirement of 4%. For example, if the FTSE All Share yields 4.3% then the average dividend yield needs to be above 4.0% (which is the minimum of 5.3% and 4%).

Value companies should have an average dividend yield above 3%. This allows value companies to earn a dividend that can keep pace with long-term inflation, while waiting for their true value to be recognised.

Sector comparison of dividend yield

Some sectors tend to have higher yields than others. It is worth comparing a company's dividend yield to others in its peer group. A company that has a dividend yield significantly higher than its sector average may be more inclined to cut the dividend if it runs into trouble, as it can afford to lower the dividend and remain attractive to investors. Remove companies from the shortlist that have dividend yields that are more than double the sector average.

Example

Table 6.3 shows the dividend yield of XP Power based on a share price of 2130p. The current dividend yield is 3.7% (= 78 ÷ 2130); broker consensus expects this to rise to 3.9% in 2018 and 4.1% in 2019, as the dividend grows.

The current dividend yield of 3.7% is above the sector average of 2.3%. At only 1.6 (= 3.7 ÷ 2.3) times the sector dividend yield, it is not so far above the sector average to be of concern.

Table 6.3 Dividend yield – XP Power

Ratio	2017	2018 (f)	2019 (f)	Sector
Dividend Yield	3.7	3.9	4.1	2.3

(f) indicates broker forecasts, taken at December 2018.

Dividend checks for growth companies

It is desirable for growth companies to pay a dividend because it helps reinforce financial discipline – the company must have the cash to pay the dividend. Your preference should be to invest in those with a dividend yield above 1%. However, a low dividend yield is desirable for growth companies as management should be aiming to reinvest most of its retained earnings into the business to maximise its earnings growth.

Summary

Key dividend checks are summarised as follows:

Dividends checks for income and value companies

- The dividend is progressively increasing over time.

- Dividend cover is above 1.5.

- Broker consensus expects dividends to rise over the next two years.

- The dividend outlook in the annual statement has a commitment to growing the dividend over time.

- The average dividend yield over the next five years should be 1% above the FTSE All Share dividend yield up to a maximum of 4% for income shares and above 3% for value companies.

- Dividend yield is less than two times the sector dividend yield.

Dividend check for growth companies

- For growth companies, the dividend yield should be above 1%.

CHAPTER 7

DEBT AND SOLVENCY CHECKS

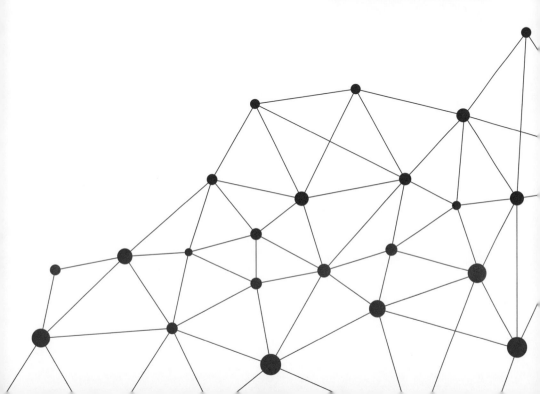

Introduction

THE BALANCE SHEET is an important consideration when investing in a company because it reflects what the company owns (assets) and owes (liabilities). It provides a snapshot of how much debt the company has, whether the company might experience financial distress and the funds it generates. This chapter discusses how to assess whether debt is manageable and ensure that the company is solvent.

Debt levels

Companies with high levels of debt are a concern for investors because there is the danger that the company has borrowed too much and will struggle to make repayments, or at least have to redirect cash that would otherwise have gone into growing the business.

A commonly cited reason for dividend cuts is the need to redirect cash to improve the position of the balance sheet, which is code for having too much debt. You will want to check that the level of debt for each company is not too high, which could cause future financial problems for the company.

Net borrowing

Net borrowing (or net debt) is the total amount of money borrowed for financing activities. This can include short- and long-term notes, as well as other payable accounts. Net borrowing is total debt minus cash and cash equivalents. The amount shows the outstanding debt the company would owe if all available cash was used to pay debts owed.

Examining the changes in net borrowing helps to understand how a business is performing financially. If net borrowing is increasing it could be a warning sign that the company is in a poor financial position, as debt is increasing relative to cash holdings. Conversely, falling net borrowing could indicate an improving financial position as debt is being paid off.

Net borrowing to EBITDA

Earnings before interest, taxes, depreciation and amortisation (EBITDA) is net profits with interest, taxes, depreciation and amortisation added back to it. It is a useful measure of earnings as it eliminates the effects of financing and accounting decisions.

The net borrowing to EBITDA ratio is a measure of leverage. It is defined as net borrowing divided by EBITDA. The ratio shows how many years it would take for a company to pay back its debt if net borrowing and EBITDA are held constant.

Morningstar has historic data on net borrowing and EBITDA on the balance sheet or income statement located in the financial section of the company profile. You can use this information to calculate the historic net borrowing to EBITDA ratios over time and examine the trend.

Companies that have net borrowing to EBITDA ratios that are trending above 2 should generally be avoided. If current net borrowing to EBITDA ratios are above 4 then the company is overburdened by debt and should be excluded from consideration.

Example

Table 7.1 shows net borrowing for XP Power has been on a declining trend since 2008 and moved into a net positive cash position in 2014 (indicated by a negative net borrowing figure). Since then, the net borrowing/EBITDA ratio has remained low, a positive for XP Power.

Table 7.1 Net borrowing/EBITDA calculation – XP Power

	2008	2009	2010	2011	2012	2013	2014	2015	2016	2017
Net Borrowing (£m)	27.8	18.7	18.4	18.6	10.6	3.5	-1.6	3.7	-4.1	8.8
EBITDA (£m)	10.0	11.2	21.6	27.5	23.4	26.2	27.1	29.5	32.1	38.6
Net Borrowing/ EBITDA	2.8	1.7	0.9	0.7	0.5	0.1	-0.1	0.1	-0.1	0.2

EV/EBITDA

Enterprise value (EV) reflects the claim on a company from both its equity holders and the owners of its debt. This provides a fuller picture of the value being put on a company compared with market capitalisation, which just looks at the claim from its equity holders. It is calculated by adding market capitalisation to net borrowing (which is total debt minus cash).

The EV/EBITDA ratio shows how many years it would take for a company to buy the claims on the company if EV and EBITDA (cash profits) are held constant. It is defined as EV divided by EBITDA.

Investors should prefer a company with an EV/EBITDA ratio below 12. Any ratio above this will signal that the company offers poor value. If the ratio is above 25 then the company is likely to be very expensive and should not be invested in.

The current EV/EBITDA ratio can also be compared against the historic trend. If the current EV/EBITDA is well above trend, it may be sensible to avoid investing in the company until its share price falls sufficiently.

Example

Table 7.2 shows the EV/EBITDA ratios for XP Power. The company's current EV/EBITDA ratio is 9.2, which is below 12, and the historic EV/ EBITDA ratio ranges from 5.3 to 17.3 from 2008 to 2017.

XP Power's valuation gradually became more expensive in 2017, with the EV/EBITDA ratio reaching 17.3 at the end of December. This would have prohibited an investment in the company at the end of 2017 or the first half of 2018. However, a subsequent fall in the share price over the second half of 2018 means that the shares are no longer prohibitively expensive.

Table 7.2 EV/ EBITDA ratios – XP Power

	2008	2009	2010	2011	2012	2013	2014	2015	2016	2017
EBITDA (£m)	10.0	11.2	21.6	27.5	23.4	26.2	27.1	29.5	32.1	38.6
Market Capitalisation (£m)	25.4	85.6	200.5	179.9	194.1	305.8	269.0	279.4	334.0	659.8
Net Borrowing (£m)	27.8	18.7	18.4	18.6	10.6	3.5	-1.6	3.7	-4.1	8.8
Enterprise Value (£m)	53.2	104.3	218.9	198.5	204.7	309.3	267.4	283.1	329.9	668.6
EV/EBITDA	5.3	9.3	10.1	7.2	8.7	11.8	9.9	9.6	10.3	17.3

Net gearing

Net gearing is another measure of a company's financial leverage. It is defined as net borrowings divided by shareholder equity (where shareholder equity is total assets minus total liabilities). Morningstar provides historic data to calculate net gearing on the balance sheet, which can be found in the financial section of the company profile.

If net gearing is trending above two thirds, investing in the company should be considered with caution as debt is a high proportion of shareholder equity. In this case, a careful assessment of debt in the industry the company belongs to should be made.

For example, many utility companies have high levels of debt with net gearing above 75%, which is generally viewed as acceptable given the large value of assets they hold and their ability to generate a reliable income from their captive customer base. Therefore, higher debt levels may be acceptable in some instances, such as utilities. In general though, companies with net gearing above two thirds should be excluded from consideration.

Example

Net gearing for XP Power is shown in table 7.3. Net gearing has been gradually declining since 2008 and turned negative in 2014, indicating that XP Power can pay all outstanding debt and still have cash left over. Borrowing increased in 2017 to fund an acquisition, but net gearing remains low.

Table 7.3 Net gearing – XP Power

	2008	2009	2010	2011	2012	2013	2014	2015	2016	2017
Net Borrowing (£m)	27.8	18.7	18.4	18.6	10.6	3.5	-1.6	3.7	-4.1	8.8
Shareholder Equity (£m)	28.8	29.6	42.6	55.6	61.1	69.2	80.2	88.3	106.1	116.0
Net Gearing (%)	96.5	63.2	43.2	33.5	17.3	5.1	-2.0	4.2	-3.9	7.6

If gearing is high, look at short-term debt as a proportion of total debt. If the ratio is high, it is a warning signal that a large proportion of debt is coming due for payment and that debt covenants will need to be re-negotiated or paid off with a new loan. The uncertainty over substantial debt can lead to a sell-off in the company, causing the share price to collapse. The short-term viability of the company also needs to be questioned.

The Morningstar website provides figures on total borrowing (i.e., total debt) and a breakdown of when that debt becomes due on the balance sheet.

Example

Table 7.4 shows total debt for XP Power and debt due to be paid within the next year. Total debt peaked in 2008 and has been paid down to low levels. Total debt for 2017 stands at £24m, which is longer term debt taken on to finance an acquisition. This debt is more than manageable given revenues of £166.8m in 2017 and cash profits of £38.6m.

Table 7.4 Total debt – XP Power

	2008	2009	2010	2011	2012	2013	2014	2015	2016	2017
Total Borrowing (£m)	31.2	22.7	23.4	24.9	14.7	8.5	2.5	8.6	5.5	24.0
Due <1 Year (£m)	7.3	3.9	12.7	13.4	7.3	8.5	2.5	4.0	5.5	0.0
Due <1 Year (%)	23.4	17.2	54.3	53.8	49.7	100.0	100.0	46.5	100.0	0.0

Solvency ratios

Solvency ratios examine whether a company has enough cash and assets to continue operating over the next year without running into financial trouble.

Current ratio

The current ratio measures a company's ability to meet its short-term obligations. It is defined as current assets (i.e., assets that can be readily converted to cash within 12 months in the normal course of business) divided by current liabilities (i.e., liabilities due within the next 12 months).

Current assets include cash, accounts receivable, inventory, marketable securities, pre-paid expenses and other liquid assets that can be readily converted to cash. The higher the current ratio the better the short-term financial position of the company.

If the ratio is less than 1, it raises concerns over whether the company can meet its short-term obligations, as current liabilities are larger than current assets. However, it doesn't necessarily mean that the company will go bankrupt. If a company has a low current ratio year after year, it could be a characteristic of the industry it operates in. For example, in the fast-food industry, the inventory turns over much more rapidly than the accounts payable becoming due, so fast-food companies tend to have low current ratios that are below 1.

Morningstar provides a history for the current ratio on the balance sheet in the financial section of the company profile.

If the current ratio is below 1, you should look at the yearly history; if the ratios are persistently below 1, it is likely to be the industry the company operates in rather than a potential solvency issue. This can also be confirmed by comparing the current ratio against companies in the same sector. In general, you should prefer companies with a current ratio above 1 with an improving trend.

Example

Table 7.5 shows solvency ratios for XP Power, including the current ratio. The current ratio has consistently been well above 1 and was a healthy 3.3 in 2017. XP Power can comfortably meet its short-term obligations.

Table 7.5 Solvency ratios – XP Power

	2008	2009	2010	2011	2012	2013	2014	2015	2016	2017
Current Ratio	1.6	1.7	1.3	1.7	1.9	1.9	2.5	2.7	2.5	3.3
Quick Ratio	0.8	1.0	0.7	0.9	1.0	1.0	1.2	1.3	1.3	1.8
Interest Cover	5.6	10.7	32.8	42.2	42.2	78.3	240.0	254.0	275.0	163.5

Current assets are important to the company because they are used to fund day-to-day operations and pay ongoing expenses. An issue with the current ratio is that it doesn't make an allowance for how illiquid some of the assets are. For example, if inventory takes a long time to sell or accounts receivable is taking several months for the company to recover on average, then the current ratio may not be a good measure of solvency.

Quick ratio

The quick ratio is a more conservative version of the current ratio. It measures a company's ability to meet its short-term obligations with its most liquid assets. It excludes inventory, which can be more difficult to sell and turn into cash. It is defined as current assets minus inventory divided by current liabilities.

Like with the current ratio, your preference should be to have a quick ratio above 1 with an improving trend. In addition, a comparison between current and quick ratio is useful; if the current ratio is significantly higher than the quick, it indicates a company's current assets are dependent on inventory.

Example

Table 7.5 shows the historic quick ratio for XP Power, which has steadily improved since 2010 and been above 1 since 2014. The quick ratio for 2017 is 1.8. As this is lower than the current ratio, it indicates that a large chunk of the current assets are inventory. Since this doesn't seem to be hampering the company, the quick ratio suggests that XP Power does not have a solvency issue.

Interest cover

Interest cover is a ratio used to determine how easily a company can pay the interest on outstanding debt. It is defined as the company's earnings before interest and taxes (EBIT) divided by interest expenses. The lower the ratio, the more the company is burdened by debt expense. Morningstar provides a history of interest cover on the balance sheet.

Interest coverage is considered healthy if it is in excess of 3, as the company is able to pay the net interest on its debt for the foreseeable future. If the interest cover is trending below 3, consider removing the company from consideration. When a company's interest cover is 1.5 or lower, its ability to meet interest expenses is questionable. If it is below 1, the company is having trouble generating enough cash flow to meet interest expenses and could easily fall into bankruptcy if its earnings suffer.

Example

The historic interest cover for XP Power is shown in table 7.5. Interest cover is well above 3 and has been in triple digits since 2014. The interest cover for 2017 currently stands at a very healthy 163.5.

Altman Z-score

The Altman Z-score was explained in detail in chapter 2. It is a model-based indicator about whether (non-financial) companies are likely to become financially distressed. A score below 1.8 means the company has a high probability of becoming distressed, while a score between 1.8 and 3 is a grey area. Our preference is to invest in companies that have an Altman Z-score above 3. Companies with an Altman Z-score below 1.8 are normally excluded from consideration.

Although this statistic doesn't appear on Morningstar, Stockopedia lists the Altman Z-score for non-financial companies a third of the way down its company profile.

Example

Looking up XP Power's Altman Z-score on Stockopedia, we find it has a healthy score of 9.9. This indicates that there is little chance of the company going bankrupt.

Piotroski F-score

The Piotroski F-score was also covered in detail in chapter 2. The Piotroski F-score is designed to measure the financial strength of a company using available data from financial statements. Scores range from 0 to 9, with a higher score indicating better financial health. Normally a Piotroski F-score above 7 is preferred, but in some circumstances a score of 6 or more, such as for larger blue-chip companies, may be acceptable. A score of 3 or less should result in a company being removed from consideration.

Stockopedia lists the Piotroski F-score on its company profile. The nine financial tests used to build the score are also available, so you can see which tests were failed and by how much.

Example

Table 7.5 shows XP Power has a Piotroski F-score of 6, indicating that the company's financial health is improving.

Summary

Key debt and solvency checks are summarised as follows:

Debt checks

- Net borrowing trend is stable or falling.

- Net borrowing to EBITDA is below 2 and on an improving or stable trend.

- Company net gearing is either less than 75% or less than sector competitors' net gearing.

- EV/EBITDA is below 12.

Solvency checks

- Current ratio and quick ratio are above 1.

- Interest cover is above 3 and the yearly trend is stable or improving.

- The Altman Z-score is above 3, indicating that the company has a low probability of bankruptcy.

- Piotroski F-score is above or equal to 6, indicating that the company's balance sheet is broadly improving.

CHAPTER 8

COMPETITIVE-
ADVANTAGE
CHECKS

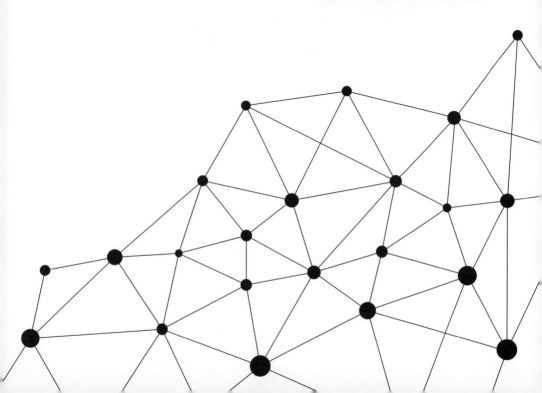

Introduction

C OMPANIES WITH A durable competitive advantage thrive because they can compete effectively and deal with market pressure. Accounting numbers can be used to see if the company is likely to have some form of competitive advantage. This chapter discusses key numbers to look at and how to interpret them.

Return on capital and equity employed

Recall from chapter 2 that return on capital employed (ROCE) measures the return generated by a company on the capital available (including long-term borrowing), while return on equity (ROE) measures the rate of profit earned by a company for its shareholders. Companies with a strong, durable competitive advantage can generate high ROCE and ROE compared with their peer group.

Morningstar provides a history of ROCE and ROE on the balance sheet or ratios page of the financial section.

For income and value companies, check whether the company's five-year average ROCE and five-year average ROE are above 10%. For growth companies, an average ROCE and average ROE above 15% is acceptable, but above 20% is preferred. Avoid investing in companies with consistently low, single digit ROCE and ROE. Ideally, the trend in ROCE and ROE should be stable or on a gradually rising trend.

Example

Table 8.1 shows the historic returns achieved on capital and equity by XP Power. ROE is consistently above 20%, while ROCE has remained above 20% since 2010, which suggests the company has a competitive advantage. ROCE averaged 23.9% and ROE averaged 24.9% over the past five years.

Table 8.1 Return on capital and equity employed – XP Power

	2008	2009	2010	2011	2012	2013	2014	2015	2016	2017
ROCE (%)	17.2	14.6	31.1	33.7	22.9	26.4	26.0	22.8	21.4	23.0
ROE (%)	30.1	25.3	43.8	41.3	26.6	27.9	26.0	23.4	21.9	25.5

Operating margin

Companies with a durable competitive advantage tend to have reliably higher profit margins, as they can consistently set a price above cost. Morningstar lists the operating margin history on the ratio page in the financial section.

Companies with a competitive advantage will normally have operating margins above 20%. Operating margins below 10% indicate that the company has no sustainable competitive advantage. Check that the current operating margin and the five-year average operating margin are above 10%. Ideally the trend in operating margin should be stable or gradually improving. Avoid companies with operating margins in low single digits.

Example

Table 8.2 shows the operating profit margins for XP Power. While margins have been above 20% since 2010, this dropped to just below 20% in 2017. However, the operating margin averaged 22.2% over the past five years, suggesting that XP Power has a competitive advantage.

Table 8.2 Profit margins – XP Power

	2008	2009	2010	2011	2012	2013	2014	2015	2016	2017
Operating Margin (%)	12.1	14.3	21.5	24.4	22.5	23.2	23.7	23.4	21.2	19.6

Consistency score

Companies with a durable competitive advantage will normally be profitable and have steadily growing sales, earnings and dividends. A consistency score measures how consistently the company has made a profit, paid a dividend and grown revenues, profits and dividends.

For a company with ten years of history the score lies between 0 and 50, with a high score indicating a more reliable company. Looking at the ten-year history for EPS, every positive year scores 1 point. Then, looking at the ten-year history of dividend per share (DPS), score 1 point for every year the company paid a dividend. Next, look at the ten-year histories for normalised EPS, revenue and DPS and score 1 point for every year a new high is reached in each of the series. (Note that the first observation is counted as a new high if it is positive.) Adding up the points gives the consistency score.

This score is usually converted into a percentage as not every company will have ten years of data readily available. When ten years of data is available the percentage consistency score is calculated by dividing the consistency score by 50. If there are fewer years, the denominator is the number of years available multiplied by five.

Consider eliminating companies that have a consistency score of 25 or less (or less than 50% if converted to a percentage). You should generally prefer companies with a consistency score of 40 or more (or more than 80% if converted to a percentage).

Example

Table 8.3 Consistency score data – XP Power

	2008	2009	2010	2011	2012	2013	2014	2015	2016	2017
Reported EPS (p)	46.5	39.4	83.9	107.1	81.7	95.8	102.1	103.7	112.0	148.3
Normalised EPS (p)	46.4	39.3	83.2	106.4	81.3	95.1	101.1	102.8	111.2	146.0
Dividend per share (DPS) (p)	17.2	18.0	27.1	36.9	41.0	45.1	50.0	54.1	71.0	78.0
Revenue (£m)	69.3	67.3	91.8	103.6	93.9	101.1	101.1	109.7	129.8	166.8

Table 8.3 shows the ten years of data required to calculate the consistency score for XP Power.

Reported EPS is positive over the ten years, which scores 10 points. A dividend was also paid every year, scoring an additional 10 points. Normalised EPS makes a new high in 2008, 2010, 2011, 2016 and 2017, scoring 5 points. DPS has progressively risen over the past ten years, scoring a further 10 points. Revenue made new highs in 2008, 2010, 2011, 2015, 2016 and 2017, scoring 6 points.

The consistency score is therefore 41 (= 10 + 10 + 5 + 10 + 6) or 82% (= 41 ÷ 50), indicating that XP Power is reliably profitable with some room to improve further.

The consistency score can also be calculated using two years of broker forecasts. Table 8.4 shows the data required to calculate the forward consistency score for XP Power. Reported EPS is positive over the ten years, including forecasts, scoring 10 points. A dividend is paid out every year, scoring an additional 10 points. Normalised EPS makes a new high in 2010, 2011, 2016, 2017, 2018 and 2019, scoring 6 points. DPS rises every year, scoring a further 10 points. Revenue made new highs in 2010, 2011, 2015, 2016, 2017, 2018 and 2019, scoring 7 points.

The consistency score is therefore 43 (= 10 + 10 + 6 + 10 + 7) or 86% (= 43 ÷ 50). XP Power's ability to reliably grow and be profitable is expected to improve over 2018 and 2019, as the prospective currency score of 86% is higher than the current consistency score of 82%.

Table 8.4 Consistency score with broker forecasts – XP Power

	2010	2011	2012	2013	2014	2015	2016	2017	2018 (f)	2019 (f)
Reported EPS (p)	83.9	107.1	81.7	95.8	102.1	103.7	112.0	148.3	167.2	193.6
Normalised EPS (p)	83.2	106.4	81.3	95.1	101.1	102.8	111.2	146.0	176.0	189.5
Dividend per share (DPS) (p)	27.1	36.9	41.0	45.1	50.0	54.1	71.0	78.0	82.5	87.5
Sales (£m)	91.8	103.6	93.9	101.1	101.1	109.7	129.8	166.8	199.0	212.8

(f) indicates broker forecasts, taken at December 2018.

Relative strength

Growth companies with strong fundamentals should be performing better than the market average. This is a sign that the market is starting to appreciate the qualities of the company. You therefore want to ensure that share price appreciation for growth companies is strong relative to rises in a benchmark market price index. (For the UK, the benchmark is typically the FTSE All Share index.)

Positive relative strength highlights shares that have recently been performing better than the market benchmark. For growth companies, you should require the three- and 12-month relative strengths to be positive, with the 12-month strength being greater than the three-month. This indicates that the share price is still growing strongly relative to the overall market, but that the share price is not running ahead too quickly. Positive one-month relative strength is a bonus.

Example

Table 8.5 shows the relative strength of growth for Bloomsbury Publishing towards the end of December 2018.

Table 8.5 Relative strength – Bloomsbury Publishing

Relative Strength	%
1 Month	2.3
3 Months	5.3
1 Year	23.5

The share price has been rising relative to the market, with relative strength being positive over one, three and 12 months. Relative strength over three months was 5.3%, compared with 23.5% over the past year. This suggests there is positive relative strength and that there is room for this to continue.

Summary

Companies with a competitive advantage will normally exhibit strong financial numbers. Look for:

- Five-year average and current ROCE and ROE above 10% for income and value companies, and above 15% for growth companies.

- Trend in ROCE and ROE is stable or is on a gradually rising trend.

- High current and five-year average operating margins that exceed 20%.

- Consistency score of 80% or higher.

- For growth companies, relative price strength is positive for three and 12 months; 12-month strength is greater than three-month strength.

CHAPTER 9

BOOK PRICE AND VALUATION RATIOS

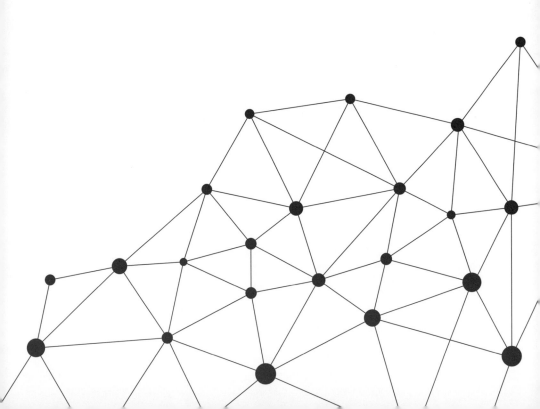

Introduction

V<small>ALUATION RATIOS ARE</small> useful as they help assess both the likely risk of an investment and the expectations the market has about its future. While previous chapters have discussed valuation measures based on earnings, sales and dividends, this chapter discusses book value ratios and how to reach a comprehensive view of valuation based on a broad spectrum of valuation ratios.

Book value

Tangible book value (also referred to as net asset value (NAV)) refers to the company's assets minus its liabilities. It excludes intangible assets, such as goodwill, brand names, etc.

Book value measure is most suitable for companies that have a great number of high-value assets or an asset-intensive business, such as utilities and telephone companies, where a large amount of infrastructure is required.

Measuring value based on asset value is particularly useful for property companies (property being an illiquid asset class) and financial organisations, such as banks and insurance companies (where most assets and liabilities are constantly valued at market prices).

Net asset value per share (NAV ps)

Net asset value per share (NAV ps) is tangible book value divided by number of shares outstanding. You want to see this figure rising over time, to indicate increasing value. Morningstar provides a history of NAV ps on the ratios segment of its company profile.

Example

Table 9.1 shows the NAV ps for XP Power, which turned positive in 2010 and has risen since then. Over the period, XP Power has been able to increase the value of the company.

Table 9.1 Net asset value per share – XP Power

	2008	2009	2010	2011	2012	2013	2014	2015	2016	2017
NAV ps (p)	-24.4	-31.4	33.8	93.0	119.5	156.4	208.9	211.0	278.8	272.7

Price to tangible book value (PTBV)

Price to tangible book value (PTBV) is current share price divided by tangible book value per share. (Tangible book value per share is tangible book value divided by the average number of shares in issue.) This measure looks at the value the market places on the book value of the company. The lower the PTBV ratio, the more likely the company is good value.

Morningstar quotes the PTBV figure in the ratios section of the company profile. A PTBV below 1 means that if the company was sold and the proceeds distributed, shareholders would receive more than the price of their shares. While this is the ideal, companies with a PTBV below 2 also offer good value. Companies with a PTBV above 10 are likely to be expensive and should be avoided.

It is worth noting that PTBV is inappropriate for some companies. Companies that do not have significant assets on the balance sheet (such as service companies and those that rely on intellectual property) are not capital-intensive, which would inflate the PTBV. Similarly, PTBV should not be used for companies that have made a recent acquisition, as this will typically increase book value and lower PTBV because the new assets go on the balance sheet at the full price paid. Therefore PTBV is not a good value measure for these types of companies.

As a general rule, exclude companies that have a PTBV greater than 1.5 times the PTBV of the sector average.

Example

The PTBV for XP Power are shown in table 9.2. At the end of 2017, the PTBV is 12.6. This is above 10, which indicates that the shares are expensive. However, XP Power made an acquisition in 2017, which partially inflated the PTBV. Towards the end of December 2018, the current PTBV fell to 7.8, based on a share price of 2130p.

Table 9.2 Price to tangible book value (PTBV) – XP Power

	2008	2009	2010	2011	2012	2013	2014	2015	2016	2017
PTBV	-	-	30.8	10.1	8.4	10.2	6.7	6.9	6.2	12.6

ROE is a useful companion metric for PTBV. A high ROE normally accompanies a high PTBV ratio because investors naturally bid up the price of a company that gives them a better return on their equity. Likewise, companies that have high earnings growth rates generally have high PTBV ratios, as investors expect the NAV ps to grow. However, a company with a high PTBV ratio and a low ROE indicates that earnings growth may not be translating into shareholder value. This type of company is more at risk of a collapse in its share price.

Combining valuation ratios

Table 9.3 shows a summary of ratios and a general guide on what the numbers mean. Note that the interpretation of these numbers is meant as a rule of thumb rather than a definitive rule; some valuation measures may be inappropriate for a particular company, or an adjustment to the general levels may be needed to account for specific characteristics of a company.

In general, companies with multiple valuation measures that are 'too good to be true' or are expensive and classified as 'poor value' or 'avoid' should be excluded from consideration as these often prove to be bad investments. Reducing the number of bad investments can help you avoid large losses, which has a beneficial effect on portfolio performance.

Table 9.3 Valuation measures

Ratio	Too good to be true	Excellent value	Good value	Average	Poor value	Avoid
Price/ Earnings (PE)	≤ 5	5 - 10	10 - 15	15 - 20	20 - 40	≥ 40
Price Earnings Growth (PEG)	≤ 0.3	0.3 - 1	1 - 1.5	1.5 - 2	≥2	No PEG
Dividend Yield	≥ 8%	5% - 8%	4% - 5%	2% - 4%	1% - 2%	≤ 1%
Dividend Cover	N/A	≥ 5	1.5 - 5	1 - 1.5	1 - 0.5	≤ 0.5
ROCE	≥ 100%	50% - 100%	20% - 50%	10% - 20%	5% - 10%	≤ 5%
Price to Tangible Book Value (PTBV)	≤ 0.25	0.25 - 1	1 - 2	2 - 5	5 - 10	≥ 10

Ratio	Too good to be true	Excellent value	Good value	Average	Poor value	Avoid
Price/Cash Flow (PCF)	≤ 5	5 - 10	10 - 15	15 - 20	20 - 40	≥ 40
Price/Sales (PSR)	≤ 0.1	0.1 - 1	1 - 3	3 - 5	5 - 20	≥ 20
Relative Strength	≥ 100%	50% - 100%	10% - 50%	-10% to 10%	-10% to -50%	≤ -50%
EPS growth	≥ 100%	30% - 100%	20% - 30%	5% - 20%	0% - 5%	≤ 0%
Net Borrowing / EBITDA	N/A	Positive net cash	0 - 1	1 - 2	2 - 4	≥ 4
EV/EBITDA	≤ 3	3 - 5	5 - 7	7 - 12	12 - 25	≥ 25
Net Gearing	N/A	≤ 0%	0% - 50%	50% - 75%	75% - 200%	≥ 200%

Example

Table 9.4 shows the current valuation scores for XP Power at the end of December 2018. The majority of the indicators suggest that XP Power currently offers good value. The share price has been falling over the second half of 2018. Once the downward price trend reverses, XP Power is likely to offer healthy returns.

Table 9.4 Valuation measures – XP Power

	Current Score	Value
PE Ratio	14.6	Good
PEG Ratio	0.5	Excellent
Dividend yield (%)	3.7	Average
Dividend cover	1.9	Good
ROCE (%)	23.0	Good
PTBV	7.8	Avoid
PCF	14.0	Average
PSR	2.5	Good
Relative Strength (3m) (%)	-17.3	Poor
EPS Growth (%)	20.6	Good
Net Borrowing / EBITDA	0.2	Good
EV / EBITDA	9.2	Average
Net Gearing (%)	7.6	Good

Summary

Book value checks are summarised as follows:

- NAV ps is stable or increasing over time.
- PTBV is less than 10.

Examining multiple valuation ratios provides a general impression of the value a company offers. Avoiding companies that have multiple extreme valuation measures helps to limit losses and improve overall portfolio performance.

CHAPTER 10

QUALITATIVE ANALYSIS

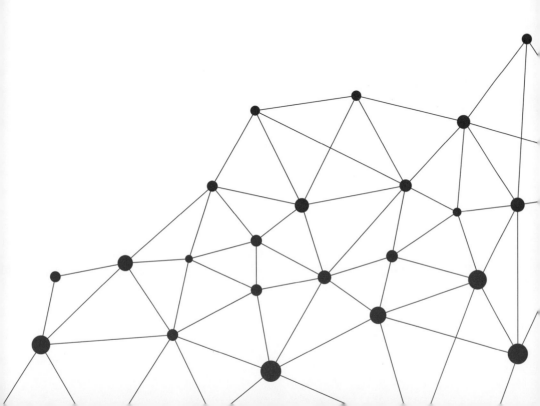

Introduction

P REVIOUS CHAPTERS HAVE shown how to narrow down the universe of listed companies based on an analysis of company numbers (i.e., quantitative analysis). This chapter focuses on how to assess qualitative aspects that can influence future performance of a company, which helps to further narrow down the list of investable companies.

Qualitative analysis helps to identify the strengths, weaknesses, opportunities and threats to a company using descriptive information. If a positive narrative about the company is built up from this analysis it will ultimately provide greater confidence to invest in the company. Conversely, if negative company risks are identified, it may deter or limit any investment made.

Financial news

The easiest place to start is to look at what other analysts and commentators are saying about a company. This gives you the opportunity to quickly find out what others think before doing more in-depth research. There are various places to find financial news:

Investors Chronicle

The *Investors Chronicle* (IC) website (www.investorschronicle.co.uk) contains commentary on small and large companies listed in the UK. It is a useful place to start your research. Searching a company name on the website provides a link to their summary page.

This summary page presents its own view on whether a company's shares are currently a buy, hold or sell. Ideally the shares you are considering should be buy rated. If shares are rated a hold or sell you will need to take a careful look at the weaknesses and threats to the company, to see if they are sufficient to deter you from investing.

The page also links to financial news articles on the IC and *Financial Times*. IC articles typically start with the pros and cons of investing in a company and then offer an explanation of their views. Normally the aim of an article is to provide a balanced view, as well as an opinion. If the company shares are rated a sell, you can normally discover the reasons.

From the summary page, you can access several other useful sections.

The profile section includes a short overview of what a company does as well as any mergers and acquisitions that are in the process of being made. A list of peers provides a quick way to identify competitors to research when looking to gain insight into the industry the company operates in. A section on institutional investors reveals who the largest investors are and the size of their positions – it is reassuring if the top shareholders own more than 10%.

The directors and dealings section lists the company executives with a biography and how long they have been with the company. Alongside this is information on the purchase and sale of shares in the company bought by the executives.

The forecasts section shows current analyst views on whether shares are a buy and how this has changed over time. They also provide price forecasts for the next 12 months, which can be a useful frame of reference. (The next two chapters discuss broker and long-term valuations in more detail and how to make best use of them.)

Financial Times and Bloomberg

The *Financial Times* (www.ft.com) and *Bloomberg* (www.bloomberg.com) websites provide a range of articles on companies. (They are typically less informative about smaller companies.) Searching for information on the sector and industry of a company on these websites can be a good way to gain a quick feel for the environment the company is currently operating in. Look for information on whether there is growth in the sector and what challenges are facing the industry.

Google financial news and Google search

Google finance (finance.google.com) collates the latest available information published online about most companies. This includes the latest official press notices as well as articles that may have been written on websites and blogs. Searching the company name or its ticker in Google tends to bring up a wider range of articles on the company, which can be informative as they tend to go back several years.

Bulletin boards

Investment bulletin boards are websites where users can post comments on companies and reply to other users' postings. Investment bulletin boards include ADVFN (www.advfn.co.uk) and Motley Fool (www.motleyfool.co.uk), where you can create a user account and access the boards for free.

The bulletin boards allow you to look up threads on a company and read about other investors' views. The threads often contain links to interesting articles, which are discussed further in the thread, that you might otherwise miss. These boards are interactive, so allow you to post your own thoughts and ask questions that you might have.

That said, contributions are mostly made by non-professional people interested in investment, so it is worth treating information provided on these boards with some scepticism. However, you can normally verify comments by reviewing other sources of information, including information provided by the company itself.

Company website and annual reports

The company website is usually a treasure trove of information about how the company is run and their general management philosophy. Annual reports will normally be available in the investor relations portion of the website.

The next sections highlight some of the more important qualitative factors that you should focus on as you read the consolidated company reports and investor material.

Business model

A business model refers to what a company does and how it makes money. It is important to understand the business model before you make an investment as otherwise you will not be able to identify the key drivers of future growth. This would leave your investment vulnerable to large losses from negative business shocks that might have been avoidable.

Source of sales and profits

The first step towards understanding any company is to work out what business interests the company has; it might focus on a single business, or it may have substantial interests in several businesses. List these businesses and look at what products and services they offer. It should be possible to determine the various business activities of a company from its annual company reports.

Look at sales and earnings for each business and ascertain which activities are currently the most important by size. You want to make sure that the key business activities are profitable. Where business activities are unprofitable, you need to understand why this is and whether it's likely to change soon. For example, if the business activity is a new start-up with good growth potential and only a small part of the company, you may have fewer concerns about current unprofitability.

Discontinued operations

Sometimes losses from discontinued operations appear in the income statement. If the losses are for a significant amount you will need to identify which operations have been discontinued (comparing reports and/or commentary on the discontinued operations).

You will then need to understand why the operations were discontinued. For example, this might be because it came to the end of its natural life or the activity was better delivered in a different way. This was the case for Tesco, a UK supermarket, which sold off its US business, Fresh & Easy, because they couldn't make it profitable. After many years of trying, Tesco decided to cut their losses and focus on other more profitable areas.

Business segment analysis

Companies are required to provide a breakdown of the different parts of a business (referred to as segments). Reportable segments are determined by geographical area; business class; 10% or more contribution to revenue; profit or assets; sector differences in terms of return, risk, growth or development potential for investors. Each reportable segment is required to disclose its sales, profit, costs, net assets and associated undertakings. The totals for each segment will equal the totals shown in the consolidated accounts.

Segmental reporting provides an opportunity to identify which parts of the business are growing and which are contracting through a simple comparison of sales and earnings over the last few years. You can then look at what the company's executives have said about growth and decline in its various markets and assess how credible their comments are.

Geographic diversification

Looking at the segmented reports you can work out the percentage of sales coming from different regions or countries. Using knowledge of which countries' economies are doing well with regional exposure can give an idea of what proportion of sales is likely to be hampered by a poor economic climate; or, conversely, the proportion of sales that might benefit from a better economic climate. For example, at the height of the Eurozone crisis companies that had a large regional exposure to the Eurozone suffered during the aftermath with poor sales and profits.

Of course, this type of analysis may not always work due to company idiosyncrasies. However, it is still a useful exercise to think about, especially for retail companies.

Customer and supplier base

Using information on the company website, you need to consider who is supplying the business with resources to manufacture products or provide services. You also need to identify who the key customers are for each business and who the key competitors are. Ideally you want to avoid companies that are too dependent on one supplier or customer for the generation of a large part of its revenue. When a company is reliant on one supplier or customer, there is a greater chance of disruption to the profitability and future growth prospects of the company.

Business focus

Ideally a company should be focused on its main area of interest, focusing on businesses that naturally complement each other. This allows its management team to concentrate on what it knows and understands well. A streamlined business focus is likely to provide more opportunities to exploit potential synergies between the different business activities, which helps to lower costs and maximise profits. For example, a business-focused company can achieve cost savings by reducing duplicated services and adopting the best business processes across their businesses, which would not otherwise be achievable if the businesses operated as separate entities.

Conversely, if a company's business activities are too diverse and have operations in different areas, management may not be able to effectively organise the separate activities and maximise profits. If the businesses sell to different customer bases and/or use different suppliers, the businesses may need to continue running separately. This will mean there are fewer opportunities to exploit cost savings through synergies and economies of scale.

Furthermore, the expertise required to run the different divisions is likely to be very different, making it harder for senior management to control the direction of the overall company. This is especially true for companies with many small, obscure businesses with low profitability, as they are likely to be poorly managed or of uneconomical scale. These are the type of companies that you want to avoid as the amount of diversification is likely to be too challenging for a single management team.

Growth strategy

Company growth in sales and profits is achieved by organic growth, when a company grows from within by reinvesting some of its profits, or by acquisitive growth, when additional businesses are acquired. Both forms of growth can be healthy. However, organic growth is typically less risky as it is a natural by-product of the management's effort to run a company well. Acquisitive growth poses more challenges and is therefore perceived to be riskier.

A healthy acquisition policy is to acquire businesses that are a good fit with the existing company structure. This includes buying out competitors or acquiring businesses that offer services or products that complement the existing range of services and products. The safest areas into which a business can diversify are closely related to what it already does, so there is pre-existing expertise and infrastructure available.

When a company buys another business, it must either make the purchase with available cash or raise the capital by issuing new shares or borrowing the money. If money is borrowed, it must generate sufficient profit to repay the loan and earn a profit similar to the existing business. If shares are issued, current shareholders' holdings are diluted. This is only in the interest of shareholders if the acquired company is more profitable than the existing business, or is made to be using synergies. This is more likely to be the case if a healthy acquisition policy is followed, as management will be able to leverage their management expertise and current infrastructure.

Diversifying outside of its core area of expertise may be a sign that a company is losing its way. In theory, this type of diversification might reduce the chances of financial damage if one area of the business lags. However, in practice, it tends to present challenges and disadvantages that can hamper overall company performance.

A company that expands into a totally unrelated field is likely to have fewer opportunities to streamline business processes and fewer economies of scale to exploit. As the businesses are very different, management will most likely want to retain expertise from the original company, since company operations may require very different skill sets. (If expertise is not retained, the original management may struggle to run the company effectively and, at worst, might find themselves in possession of a business they can't run profitably.) This type of acquisition is therefore likely to incur much higher costs as additional staff and infrastructure need to be maintained. There is therefore a greater risk that high costs might impair the value of the company.

For example, if an ice cream producer takes over a car sales company, the skills to run the business are very different. The senior management would most likely want to retain the staff for both businesses, as people who make ice cream are unlikely to be able to sell cars well, and vice versa. The process used to produce and sell ice cream have no overlap with the marketing and sale of cars. The fixed assets used to produce and distribute ice cream are of no relevance to a business selling cars. Ultimately, there are next to no synergies to exploit between the two businesses, so both will have to be run independently.

In summary, you want to skew your investments to companies with a business model that is easy to understand and where management focus is on a core area of expertise. You want to avoid companies that have over-diversified into a broad range of businesses or are looking to acquire businesses outside of their core area of expertise. Where a company is in the process of acquiring a new business, a careful assessment of whether this will add value or dilute the company's profitability and growth potential needs to be made.

Future direction and outlook

A good way to assess the outlook for a company is to first evaluate the key accounting numbers (as proposed in previous chapters) to build a picture of historic performance. You can then read the comments made by the chairman and directors in the annual reports (and other investment presentations) to gain a sense of whether their comments are in line with the actual performance achieved. If the forward-looking views tally, the executives' views on the immediate future are likely to be a fair reflection of the outlook.

In bad years, you should look to see if the executives discuss the problems of the business and the mistakes made. This action should be viewed positively, as a company that is willing to identify and admit its failings is more likely to learn from and avoid these mistakes in the future. Such qualities will usually make the company a better investment, as opposed to a company that blames circumstances outside of its control, such as the weather. If the company made a large loss and statements from the chairman or directors are overly positive without addressing the underlying problems, this should raise some concerns about investing in the company.

For growth companies, if statements from the chairman or directors are pessimistic, a careful assessment of the growth story needs to be made as earnings growth may be at an end.

Competitive advantage

A company has a competitive advantage if it has attributes or abilities that are difficult to duplicate or surpass, providing it with a superior or favourable long-term position over competitors. As discussed in chapter 8, the most reliable evidence of a company with a competitive advantage is the ability of management to employ capital at a high rate of return while maintaining a high profit margin and decent free cash flow. This can be ascertained by looking at company numbers.

A company with a sustainable competitive advantage can compete effectively against its competitors while enjoying growth and profits. Thus, when a company can achieve a competitive advantage, its shareholders are likely to be well rewarded over the long term.

Conversely, a company in a sector that exhibits intense rivalry between competitors will find it hard to establish or maintain a competitive advantage and remain profitable. This problem is likely to be compounded if the products or services are easily substituted by products or services offered by competitors.

While looking at company numbers can confirm the presence of a competitive advantage, it is a useful exercise to try and articulate what these competitive advantages are and whether they are likely to continue over the medium term. Sustainable competitive advantages are essential for a company to thrive in today's competitive global environment and be successful long term.

Competitive advantages, sometimes known as business franchise or economic moats, arise in several different ways:

Cost leadership/low pricing

Cost leadership occurs when a company can offer the same quality product as its competitors at a lower price. A company's ability to deliver goods and services at low cost stems from economies of scale, operational efficiencies, proprietary technology or location, all of which allow the company to produce or sell goods in a more efficient manner.

A company that is the cheapest provider of a good or service makes it difficult for competitors to compete. This may provide sufficient pricing power, as well as competitive barriers to entry, which allow the company to generate a high return on capital over a long period of time. In addition, consistently low pricing can build brand loyalty, which is a further competitive advantage.

Cost leaders are typically large companies that have been able to exploit economies of scale to the point that they have little competition. If they are making a reasonable profit margin it is likely they are selling high volumes of common products or services that are needed at regular intervals or by most people at some point in their life. Low cost producers and sellers cover many kinds of businesses, such as insurance, furniture, groceries, carpets, etc.

Product differentiation

Low cost is only one of many factors that allow a company to compete effectively. A company that can positively differentiate its products or services by offering one or more marketable attributes (such as better quality, more features at a certain price point or better customer service) can help set them apart from their competitors. Offering a unique product or service, one that better meets the needs and desires of customers, helps build customer loyalty and is therefore less likely to lose market share to a competitor.

When assessing whether a differentiation strategy is a sustainable competitive advantage, one has to consider how easily company offerings can be imitated. If competitors can't offer the same degree of differentiation, the competitive advantage is likely to be sustainable.

Established position in niche market

A company may decide to focus on a niche market, marketing a product or service to a particular segment of the economy as opposed to the entire population. This strategy aims to gain a competitive advantage by being the cheapest provider in that segment (although not necessarily the cheapest overall) or offering tailored products or services to meet the needs of the segment better than its competitors.

For example, a large supermarket operator may open smaller outlets in inner city areas that aim to be the cheapest in the local area. However, the stores do not need to be the cheapest overall, since they can take advantage of a captive local customer base and offer customer convenience instead of the cheapest prices.

Adapting product line

A product or service that never changes can become vulnerable to competition. In contrast, a product (or service) line that can evolve by improving the existing offering, or by adding complementary products or services, can help to keep and build a loyal customer base.

For example, Apple offers regular updates to their mobile phone, tablet and computer lines which leads to a regular cycle of customers upgrading at regular intervals. In addition, for their mobile phone and tablet range, they are now starting to offer complementary devices, such as watches that help monitor fitness or interact with home appliances and cars. Combined with their iTunes store and software environment, it provides a compelling reason to stay loyal to the brand.

Excellent brands

A company that has an excellent brand offers products or services that customers are willing to pay more for because they believe the offering is of higher quality and can be trusted. A good brand is invaluable as it causes customers to prefer the brand over competitors. Being the market leader and having a great corporate reputation can be part of a powerful competitive advantage. There are lots of companies with strong brands, like Coca-Cola, Pepsi, Apple, Adidas and McDonald's, to name but a few.

Strategic assets

Another way for a business to gain a competitive advantage is to utilise strategic assets to defend revenue and profits. Strategic assets, such as patents, trade secrets, copyright and long-term contracts provide a sustainable competitive advantage by making competition illegal or very difficult. For example, pharmaceutical companies such as AstraZeneca and GlaxoSmithKline patent blockbuster drugs to prevent generic pharmaceutical companies from producing them. This allows them to recoup their R&D costs and make a profit.

Dominance in a market (tolls)

A company with both a dominant market position and exclusive control over a large share of the market has the ability to collect a toll from anyone needing that product or service. Typically, a company has the dominant market position because of economic barriers that prevent or greatly impede a potential competitor's ability to compete in the market. Economic barriers include economies of scale, capital requirements, cost advantages and technological superiority.

For example, Mastercard and American Express can charge a toll on every transaction its customers make, as they have a first-mover advantage combined with superior technology and high sunk costs. Utility companies require a large upfront investment of capital to deliver their services, which limit the number of companies in an industry. Consequently, water, electricity and telephone companies are all able to levy tolls on their users.

Strong balance sheet/cash generative

Companies with low debt and a high positive cash flow have the flexibility to take advantage of investment opportunities when they arise. They do not have to worry about gaining access to working capital, liquidity or solvency. The balance sheet is the foundation of the company, allowing it to fund future investment at low cost.

This helps provide a competitive advantage over companies with weaker balance sheets that must rely on external financing at higher cost when trying to take advantage of investment opportunities. For example, the global financial crisis meant that it was very difficult for companies to raise external finance and would have prevented companies with weak balance sheets from taking advantage of investment opportunities when they became cheap.

Switching costs

If a company plays an integral role in your life, switching to another company's product or service may not be worth the trouble. Switching costs may involve a monetary cost, but can equally take the form of costs on time, effort or social pressure.

Monetary costs may come directly in the form of an incumbent company levying a charge for switching, such as bank closure fees, or it may come indirectly through consumers having to purchase replacement add-ons and extensions for the new product or service due to incompatibility. For example, blades for Gillette razors are not compatible with Wilkinson razors, Canon's DSLR lenses are not compatible with Nikon lenses, and Apple's mobile apps can't be used on android phones. Locking customers into a product ecosystem may be an effective way to retain customers. In addition, a company may offer loyalty incentives, such as frequent flier miles, coupons or other 'membership' bonuses, which are lost if the consumer switches to a competitor.

Other switching costs include the time and effort required to transition to another product or service. For example, moving to an iMac from a PC, or switching from an iPhone to an android phone, requires a certain amount of learning before becoming a proficient user. Social factors such as brand loyalty or being part of an elite group (nobody wants to be seen using a BlackBerry device when iPhones and android phones are so superior) may also be a factor when deciding when to switch.

A company that is solely reliant on high switching costs may only have a weak competitive advantage. However, if this is combined with other competitive advantages, switching costs may help reinforce an overall sustainable competitive advantage.

When performing a detailed assessment of a company's competitive advantages you need to consider how they align with the most urgent and important needs of customers in the market, as well as the strengths and weaknesses of competitors. It is useful to try and prioritise the list of potential competitive advantages in order of likelihood of delivering a sustainable competitive advantage that can be used to differentiate the company over the longer term.

Try to articulate the most promising competitive advantages that you have identified for a company into a concise statement. This statement should ideally highlight the distinctive advantage a company has that cannot easily be replicated by others. This is a useful exercise as it helps you gain a deeper understanding of the fundamental strengths of a company, while forming a case to invest.

Management

The backbone of every successful company is a strong management team. Management is a key factor in the success of a company as it makes the strategic decisions and therefore serves a crucial function in determining the fate of the company. Great management can help steer a company to financial success as they are better able to construct and execute a good business plan, which helps achieve its main aims and goals.

Leadership

The first step in looking at management is to identify the key people running the company. This includes the chairman, chief executive officer (CEO) and chief financial officer (CFO), as well as operational managers. Every listed company has a corporate information section on its website about the management. This usually includes a biography on each executive with their employment history, educational background and any applicable achievements.

You want to see executives that have either been with the company a long time (and possibly worked their way up the business hierarchy) or have a transferable background to the company they are working for. If an executive has had a long tenure with the company, it is likely that the manager is a successful and profitable manager (as otherwise the board of directors would have made changes). What you don't want to see are executives on the board that do not have a relevant background for the company or sector they are currently working in. It is worth identifying where executives have worked previously to see how they have performed. It is a good sign if executives saw positive results during their tenure with other companies.

When a founder or chief executive has been the driving force behind a company for many years you need to consider what succession plans are in place as well as how the business will cope once the key manager steps down from that position. When the change of management happens, you need to review growth assumptions and potentially make them more conservative to reflect the loss of leadership. You should be wary of companies where the succession risk is high.

If the company has recently experienced a period of poor performance, management restructuring may be a positive sign that changes are being made in the hope of improving that outlook. However, if several changes to management have been made over the previous few years it is indicative of a company in real trouble and should therefore be avoided. A management team consisting of people who come from completely unrelated industries should raise questions about their competency.

Management discussion and analysis

Management discussion and analysis (MD&A) is the section of a company's annual report in which management discuss a broad range of different aspects of the company, both past and present.

Reading through the MD&A sections of consecutive annual reports can provide a feel for management style. You want to look for frank, worthwhile commentary on the management outlook that is refreshed at each annual report. It should be taken as a bad sign if the commentary is standardised and doesn't change much from report to report. When reading the MD&A you should try to work out whether there is a capable management team in place that is able to deliver positive results.

Ideally, management style should be open, flexible and transparent about the running of a company. Good management think and act in the best interests of the company and shareholders. They focus less on the short-term pressures and more on the long-term health of the company, following their core mission statement and business plan. Comparing what MD&A said in past years and what they are currently saying helps to gain an insight into the strategies being pursued and whether they have been implemented well.

Management should be able to demonstrate that they understand the business and their customers as well as present a realistic view of the company and the industry it operates in. Key strategic and investment decisions should be covered in the MD&A section. Management should provide a solid rationale for the decisions and strategies adopted, which should be reflected in resources being used wisely, with expenses kept under control.

A sign of good management is often more evident when a company encounters business issues and problems. Good management should communicate quickly and honestly about the problems, dealing with them as quickly as possible by making the necessary changes.

Conference calls

Every quarter or half year management will host conference calls for analysts to discuss the performance of the company. The calls are normally advertised on the investors section of the company website. (If they are not, you can email the company explaining that you are a shareholder and that you would like to be invited to future calls.) In addition, recordings of previous calls may also be made available on the website.

The first part of the conference call is usually a discussion of the company's financial results. However, the more interesting part is the question and answer portion of the call. Analysts and shareholders call in to ask questions of management, often regarding clarification over key decisions and strategies or for concerns to be addressed. The answers provided can be quite informative about the company.

In addition, these calls provide insight into management style. You should look for management providing candid, forthright answers that are easy to understand. It should raise concerns if management avoids answering questions and is generally evasive.

Management pay

It is worth checking whether the remuneration for management is excessive or not. The company's latest annual report will contain information on salary and bonuses for key management. You should beware of 'lifestyle companies', where management have been in place with large salaries for many years but where the business has performed poorly.

Shareholder ownership

Executives are compensated by cash, equity and options. It is a positive sign if members of management own a significant number of shares. The ideal situation is where the founder of the company is running the company, or it is a family-run business with a substantial shareholding. When you know that a majority of management's wealth is invested in shares, you can have greater confidence that they will operate in the interest of shareholders.

That said, you don't want to see a single person or entity with majority control over the available shares in a company as this may result in the company being run for the benefit of a small number of large shareholders who are main board directors. This can create a major conflict of interest, where minority shareholders have little influence over how the company operates. Your preference should be to invest in companies where the main board owns less than 50% of the issued share capital and where there is large institutional investment.

The exception to this guideline is where there is large ownership from a founder or it is a family-owned business where the business is being run in the shareholders' interest as a whole. That said, it's possible for companies to offer attractive investment returns where the main board controls over half of the issued share capital. You just have to be aware of the risks this poses.

Director dealings

Few people are better placed to evaluate a company's prospects than those who run it. This is why many investors regard directors' share dealings (or insider dealing, as it is sometimes referred to) as a key indicator of future prospects. If key members of the management team (such as the chairman, CEO or CFO) have all been selling large amounts of shares you should be wary of investing in the company. The *Investors Chronicle* and *FT* both contain summaries of director dealings over the past 12 months, which can be used to check whether this has happened.

Summary

The aim of qualitative research is to produce a list of strengths, weaknesses, opportunities and threats to the company you are thinking about investing in. This list should contain your thoughts about what the company does, how it makes money, the competitive advantage of the company and the effectiveness of management. This should help provide a sense of whether the company is an attractive investment.

CHAPTER 11

BROKER
VALUATIONS

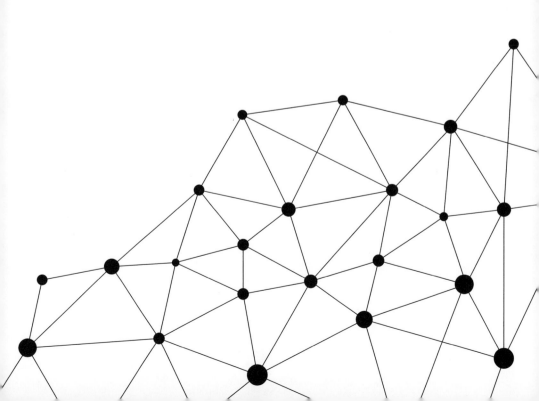

Introduction

Each company is normally followed by several brokers who produce a range of reports and analysis. A survey of broker forecasts for company revenue, earnings and dividends over the next two years can be used to form a broker consensus on fair valuation and whether brokers collectively view the shares as cheap, fairly valued or expensive.

This chapter shows how to produce an estimate of the broker's consensus price forecast for a company, based on their forecasts of the fundamentals. It then explains how to construct a price range that the shares are expected to trade in over the near term. This range is used to signal where brokers believe the current value lies.

Calculating broker valuations

Several different approaches can be employed to estimate the value brokers place on the shares of a company. This section discusses each of the individual methods in turn and then explains how to aggregate these forecasts into a single consensus price and a price range for assessing value.

Sales-based broker valuation method

The sales-based broker valuation estimates the consensus share price using brokers' consensus forecasts of sales over the next two years.

Step 1: Calculate sales per share

Sales per share is sales revenue divided by the total number of shares outstanding. While historic sales per share is easily calculated, the forecast sales per share needs an estimate of the number of outstanding shares over the next two years. To estimate the number of shares outstanding in forecast years, you can either use the current number of shares (if the number of outstanding shares has been gradually decreasing) or you can assume that the number of shares outstanding grows at a similar pace to recent history. Forecast sales per share is then calculated by dividing the consensus broker forecast for sales by the estimate of the number of shares outstanding.

Example

Sales per share, including broker forecasts, for XP Power has already been calculated in chapter 4, table 4.2. Table 11.1 reproduces the sales per share calculation, for convenience.

Table 11.1 Sales per share (SPS) calculation – XP Power

	2010	2011	2012	2013	2014	2015	2016	2017	2018 (f)	2019 (f)
Sales (£m)	91.8	103.6	93.9	101.1	101.1	109.7	129.8	166.8	199.0	212.8
Shares Outstanding (m)	19.0	19.1	19.1	19.1	19.2	19.2	19.2	19.4	19.6	19.8
Sales per Share (SPS) (p)	483.2	542.9	492.8	528.0	526.7	572.2	677.4	860.3	1014.4	1072.1

(f) indicates broker forecasts, taken at December 2018.

Step 2: Calculate price to sales ratio (PSR) measures

The price to sales ratio (PSR) is price divided by sales per share. The highest and lowest PSR in each of the past five reported years can be calculated using the highest and lowest closing price and the reported sales per share in each year. The highest/lowest PSR for a year is calculated by dividing the highest/lowest price of the year by the reported sales per share.

The average high (or low) PSR over the past five years can be calculated as an average of these highest/lowest price to sales ratios. A central average PSR is calculated as an average of the highest and lowest PSRs over the past five years. (Note that this is equivalent to taking an average of the average highest PSR and the average lowest PSR.)

Example

Table 11.2 shows the calculation of the highest and lowest PSRs for XP Power, which is also calculated in chapter 4. The highest price to sales ratio in 2017 is calculated by dividing the highest closing price in 2017 (3626.4p) by sales per share in 2017 (860.3p), which gives 4.2. The lowest price to sales ratio in 2017 is calculated by dividing the lowest closing price in 2017 (1725p) by sales per share in 2017 (860.3p), which gives 2.2. The highest and lowest PSRs in other years are calculated in a similar way.

Table 11.2 Annual price to sales ratio ranges

	2013	2014	2015	2016	2017	Average
High Price (p)	1630.0	1798.0	1750.0	1845.1	3626.4	
Low Price (p)	972.3	1340.0	1375.0	1396.8	1725.0	
Sales per Share (SPS) (p)	528.0	526.7	572.2	677.4	860.3	
PSR low	1.8	2.5	2.4	2.1	2.0	2.2
PSR high	3.1	3.4	3.1	2.7	4.2	3.3

Over the past five years, the highest PSRs have averaged 3.3 and the lowest PSRs have averaged 2.2. The overall average PSR is 2.75 (= (2.2 + 3.3) ÷ 2). The highest PSR was 4.2 in 2017 and the lowest PSR occurred in 2013, when it touched 1.8. These statistics are summarised in table 11.3.

Table 11.3 Summary statistics – price to sales ratio

	Low	Average low	Average	Average high	High
Price to sales ratio (PSR)	1.8	2.2	2.75	3.3	4.2

Step 3: Produce consensus broker price

The consensus broker target price (based on sales) for a forecast year is calculated by multiplying the average PSR by the forecast sales per share.

Example

From table 11.1, the forecast sales per share is 1014.4p in 2018 and 1072.1p in 2019. The average PSR is 2.75. Thus the target price for the end of 2018 is 2789.6p (= 2.75 × 1014.4p) and the target price for the end of 2019 is 2948.3p (= 2.75 × 1072.1p).

Step 4: Produce valuation ranges

The valuation ranges are intended to act as a guide to whether the shares look expensive or cheap based on broker consensus and possible future market valuations.

The broker view is that the shares offer good value if the current share price is below the forecast sales per share multiplied by the average low PSR, and excellent value if the share price is below the forecast sales per share multiplied by the lowest PSR. (This assessment assumes you have carried out all the quality checks and are satisfied with the results; otherwise there could be some hidden problem that justifies a low valuation.) The shares are considered poor value if the current share price is above the average high PSR multiplied by the forecast sales per share, and expensive if the current share price is above the highest PSR multiplied by the forecast sales per share.

Example

In the case of XP Power, the average low PSR is 2.2 (see table 11.3) and the sales per share are forecast to be 1014.4p in 2018 and 1072.1p in 2019. Thus the broker view would consider the shares to be good value if the share price falls below 2231.7p (= 2.2 × 1014.4p) for 2018 and 2358.6p (= 2.2 × 1072.1p) for 2019.

The lowest PSR over the past five years is 1.8. The share would be considered excellent value if the share price falls below 1825.9p (= 1.8 × 1014.4p) for 2016 and 1929.8p (= 1.8 × 1072.1p) for 2017.

From table 11.3, the average high PSR is 3.3. Thus, if the price rose to 3347.5p (= 3.3 × 1014.4p) during 2018 or 3537.9p (= 3.3 × 1072.1p) in 2019 the broker view would be that the shares offer poor value.

The highest PSR over the past five years was 4.2. Consequently, if the share price rose above 4260.5p (= 4.2 × 1014.4p) in 2018 or 4502.8p (= 4.2 × 1072.1p) in 2019, the shares would be considered expensive.

The boundaries of the price ranges are summarised in table 11.4. Towards the end of December 2018 XP Power's share price was 2130p. The shares are therefore considered to be good value based on consensus broker sales forecasts for 2018 and 2019. There is 38.4% upside to the end of 2019.

Table 11.4 Broker price ranges

	Excellent value	Good value	Average	Poor value	Expensive
2018 SPS: 1014.4p	1825.9	2231.7	2789.6	3347.5	4260.5
2019 SPS: 1072.1p	1929.8	2358.6	2948.3	3537.9	4502.8

Earnings-based broker valuation method

The earnings-based broker valuation method estimates the consensus share price using brokers' consensus forecasts of earnings over the next two years.

Step 1: Collect earnings per share data

Normalised historic EPS data and two years of broker forecasts are readily available on Morningstar and Stockopedia websites.

Example

The normalised earnings per share for XP Power, including consensus broker forecasts, is shown in table 11.5.

Table 11.5 Normalised earnings per share (EPS)

	2010	2011	2012	2013	2014	2015	2016	2017	2018 (f)	2019 (f)
Normalised EPS (p)	83.20	106.40	81.30	95.10	101.10	102.80	111.20	146.00	176.0	189.5

(f) indicates broker forecasts, taken at December 2018.

Step 2: Calculation of price to earnings ratio (PE ratio) measures

The PE ratio is price divided by earnings per share. The highest and lowest PE ratio in each of the past five reported years are calculated by using the highest and lowest closing price and the reported EPS in each year. The highest/lowest PE ratio for a particular year is calculated by dividing the highest/lowest price of the year by the reported EPS.

The average high (or low) PE ratio over the past five years can be calculated as an average of these highest (or lowest) PE ratios. A central average PE ratio is calculated as an average of the highest and lowest PE ratios over the past five years.

Example

The highest and lowest closing price in each of the past five years is the same as in the sales-based method. The highest PE ratio in 2017 is calculated by dividing the highest closing price for XP Power's shares in 2017 (3626.4p) by EPS in 2017 (146.0p), which gives 24.8.

The lowest PE ratio in 2017 is calculated by dividing the lowest closing price for XP Power's shares in 2017 (1725.0p) by EPS in 2017 (146.0p), which gives 11.8. The highest and lowest PE ratios for other years are shown in table 11.6.

Table 11.6 Annual price to earnings ratio ranges

	2013	2014	2015	2016	2017	Average
High Price (p)	1630.0	1798.0	1750.0	1845.1	3626.4	
Low Price (p)	972.3	1340.0	1375.0	1396.8	1725.0	
Normalised EPS (p)	95.1	101.1	102.8	111.2	146.0	
PSR low	10.2	13.3	13.4	12.6	11.8	12.2
PSR high	17.1	17.8	17.0	16.6	24.8	18.7

Over the past five years, the high PE ratios have averaged 18.7 (= (17.1 + 17.8 + 17.0 + 16.6 + 24.8) ÷ 5) and the low PE ratios have averaged 12.2 (= (10.2 + 13.3 + 13.4 + 12.6 + 11.8) ÷ 5). The overall average PE ratio is 15.5 (= (12.2 + 18.5) ÷ 2).

The highest PE ratio over the five years was 24.8 in 2017 and the lowest PE ratio was 10.2 in 2013. These statistics are summarised in table 11.7.

Table 11.7 Summary statistics – price to earnings ratio

	Low	Average Low	Average	Average High	High
PE Ratio (p)	10.2	12.2	15.5	18.7	24.8

Step 3: Produce consensus broker price

The consensus broker target price (based on earnings) for a forecast year is calculated by multiplying the average PE ratio by the forecast earnings per share.

Example

From table 11.5, forecast earnings per share is 176.0p in 2018 and 189.5p in 2019. The average PE ratio is 15.5. Thus, the target price for the end of 2018 is 2719.2p (= 15.5 × 176.0p) and for the end of 2019 is 2927.8p (= 15.5 × 189.5p).

Towards the end of December 2018 XP Power's share price was 2130p, which suggests that the company is trading 21.7% below broker valuation for 2018 and 27.2% below the broker valuation for 2019.

Step 4: Produce broker valuation ranges

The valuation ranges are intended as a guide to determine whether the shares look expensive or cheap based on broker earnings consensus and future market valuations.

The broker view is that the shares offer good value if the current share price is below the forecast EPS multiplied by the average low PE ratio, and excellent value if the share price is below the forecast EPS multiplied by the lowest PE ratio. If the current share price is above the average high PE ratio multiplied by the forecast EPS, the broker view is that the shares are poor value. The shares are expensive if the share price is above the highest PE ratio multiplied by the forecast EPS.

Example

In the case of XP Power, the average low PE ratio is 12.2 (see table 11.7) and EPS is forecast to be 176.0p in 2018 and 189.5p in 2019. Thus, the consensus broker view would consider the shares to be good value if the share price falls below 2147.2p (= 12.2 × 176.0p) for 2018 and 2311.9p (= 12.2 × 189.5p) for 2019.

The lowest PE ratio over the past five years is 10.2. The share would be considered excellent value if the share price falls below 1795.2p (= 10.2 × 176.0p) for 2018 and 1932.9p (= 10.2 × 189.5p) for 2019.

From table 11.7, the average high PE ratio is 18.7. Thus, if the price is above 3291.2p (= 18.7 × 176.0p) during 2018 or 3543.7p (= 18.7 × 189.5p) in 2019 the broker view is that the shares offer poor value. The broker valuation ranges for 2018 and 2019 are summarised in table 11.8.

Towards the end of December 2018 XP Power's share price was 2130p. Broker valuations based on earnings forecasts currently suggest that the share price is good value based on consensus earnings forecasts for 2018 and 2019.

Table 11.8 Broker valuation ranges

	Excellent value	Good value	Average	Poor value	Expensive
2018 EPS: 176.0p	1795.2	2147.2	2719.2	3291.2	4364.8
2019 EPS: 189.5p	1932.9	2311.9	2927.8	3543.7	4699.6

Broker target price: Hybrid sales-earnings-based broker valuation method

The hybrid sales-earnings valuation method combines broker views on future sales with information on net profit margins and the number of shares outstanding to estimate future earnings and place a value on the shares of a company.

Step 1: Obtain future sales forecasts

Broker consensus sales forecasts for the next two accounting years are the starting point of the hybrid valuation method.

Example

XP Power's broker sales forecasts towards the end of December 2018 were for sales to rise from £166.8m in 2017 to £199m in 2018 and to £212.8m in 2019.

Step 2: Estimate the average net profit margin

Profit margin is net earnings divided by sales. Equivalently, profit margin can be defined as the price to sales ratio divided by the price to earnings ratio.

To estimate the average long-term profit margin, the average PSR (calculated in step 2 of the sales-based broker valuation method) is divided by the average PE ratio (calculated in step 2 of the earnings-based broker valuation method).

Example

Table 11.3 shows that the average PSR is 2.75, while table 11.7 shows the average PE ratio is 15.5 for XP Power. Thus, the average profit margin is 17.8% (= 2.75 ÷ 15.5).

Step 3: Estimate future net earnings over the next two years

Net earnings for a year in the future are obtained by multiplying the long-term profit margin against future sales in that year. Thus, net earnings for the next accounting year are calculated by multiplying the average profit margin by the next accounting years' sales. Similarly, net earnings for the second year are the average net profit margin multiplied by the broker forecast of sales in two years' time.

Example

XP Power's sales are forecast to be £199m in 2018 and £212.8m in 2019. Thus, net earnings are estimated to be £35.4m (= 17.8% × £199m) in 2018 and £37.9m (= 17.8% × £212.8m) in 2019.

Step 4: Estimate outstanding shares in future years

The annual growth rate of outstanding shares over the past five years is calculated in the same way as the sales-based broker valuation method.

Example

The number of shares outstanding has already been estimated for XP Power in table 11.1. It is assumed that there are 19.6m shares outstanding in 2018 and 19.8m shares in 2019.

Step 5: Calculate future earnings per share

Forecast EPS is calculated by dividing forecast net earnings by the forecast number of outstanding shares.

Example

Table 11.9 shows the calculation of forecast EPS over the next two years. EPS for the reporting year 2018 is 180.6p (= (35.4 ÷ 19.6) × 100) and is estimated to be 191.4p in 2019. (Here we multiply by 100 to convert from pounds to pence.)

Table 11.9 Earnings per share (EPS) calculation incorporating additional information

		Forecasts
	2018	2019
Net earnings (£m)	35.4	37.9
Shares outstanding (m)	19.6	19.8
EPS (p)	180.6	191.4

Broker forecasts at December 2018.

Note that the consensus broker forecasts for normalised EPS are not being used in this method. Instead, the broker forecasts for future sales are being used in combination with estimates of the long-term profit margin and the number of shares outstanding to produce an alternative estimate of EPS.

Step 6: Calculate the price to earnings ratio ranges

Calculation of the PE ratio ranges follow the methodology used in step 2 of the earnings-based broker valuation method. The highest and lowest PE ratio in each of the past five reported years are calculated using the highest/lowest closing price and the reported EPS. The highest or lowest PE ratio for a year is calculated by dividing the highest/lowest price of the year by the reported earnings per share.

The average high (or low) PE ratio over the past five years is calculated as an average of these highest/lowest price to earnings ratios. A central average PE ratio is calculated as an average of the highest and lowest PE ratios over the past five years.

Example

The historic highest and lowest PE ratios in each year for XP Power are calculated in table 11.6. The PE ratio summary statistics are shown in table 11.7. For convenience, the statistics are replicated in table 11.10.

Table 11.10 Summary statistics – price to earnings ratio

	Low	Average low	Average	Average high	High
PE ratio (p)	10.2	12.2	15.5	18.7	24.8

Step 7: Calculate the consensus broker price forecast

The consensus broker target price for a forecast year is calculated by multiplying the average PE ratio by the forecast EPS.

Example

From table 11.9, the forecast EPS is 180.6p in 2018 and 191.4p in 2019. The average PE ratio is 15.5. Thus, the target price for the end of 2018 is 2790.3p (= 15.5 × 180.6p) and the target price for the end of 2019 is 2957.1p (= 15.5 × 191.4p).

Towards the end of December 2018 XP Power's share price was 2130p, which suggests that the company is trading below broker valuation for 2018 and 2019.

Step 8: Produce broker valuation ranges

The valuation ranges are intended as a guide to determine whether the shares look expensive or cheap based on broker consensus and possible future market valuations.

The broker view is that the shares offer good value if the current share price is below the forecast EPS multiplied by the average low PE ratio, and excellent value if the share price is below the forecast EPS multiplied by the lowest PE ratio.

The broker view is that the shares are poor value if the current share price is above the average high PE ratio multiplied by the forecast EPS, and expensive if the current share price is above the highest PE ratio multiplied by the forecast EPS.

Example

In the case of XP Power, the average low PE ratio is 12.2 (see table 11.10) and EPS is forecast to be 180.6p in 2018 and 191.4p in 2019. Thus, the consensus broker view is that the shares are good value if the share price is below 2203.3p (= 12.2 × 180.6p) for 2018 and 2335.1p (= 12.2 × 191.4p) for 2019.

The lowest PE ratio over the past four years was 10.2. Thus, the shares would be considered excellent value if the share price falls below 1842.1p (= 10.2 × 180.6p) for 2016 and 1952.3p (= 10.2 × 191.4p) for 2017.

From table 11.10, the average high PE ratio is 18.7. Thus, if the price is above 3377.2p (= 18.7 × 180.6p) during 2018 or 3579.2p (= 18.7 × 191.4p) in 2019 the broker view would be that the shares offer poor value.

The highest PE ratio over the past four years was 24.8. Consequently, if the share price rose above 4478.9p (= 24.8 × 180.6p) in 2018 or 4746.7p (= 24.8 × 191.4p) in 2019, the shares would be considered expensive.

Towards the end of December 2018 XP Power's share price was 2130p. Broker valuations based on hybrid forecasts currently suggest that the share price is good value for 2018 and 2019. The boundaries of the price ranges are summarised in table 11.11.

Table 11.11 Broker price target ranges

	Excellent value	Good value	Average	Poor value	Expensive
2018 EPS: 180.6p	1842.1	2203.3	2790.3	3377.2	4478.9
2019 EPS: 191.4p	1952.3	2335.1	2957.1	3579.2	4746.7

Producing a consensus broker valuation

In the examples above, the broker valuation methods can sometimes give different conclusions. In general, you would like at least two of the three methods to suggest that the company offers good value. To produce an overall broker consensus, you can either take the average value of the ranges or choose the method which has the closest (average) fair value price.

Example

Table 11.12 summarises the broker valuations for the different approaches. The consensus is obtained by finding the average value in each column of the table. The consensus broker fair value price is 2766.4p.

Towards the end of December 2018 the share price was 2130p, meaning that the overall broker consensus is that the shares offer good value. XP Power's shares would be excellent value if the price fell below 1821.1p and poor value if the price rises above 3338.6p a share.

Table 11.12 Composite consensus broker valuation – end 2018 forecast

	Excellent value	Good value	Average	Poor value	Expensive
Sales	1825.9	2231.7	2789.6	3347.5	4260.5
Earnings	1795.2	2147.2	2719.2	3291.2	4364.8
Hybrid	1842.1	2203.3	2790.3	3377.2	4478.9
Average	**1821.1**	**2194.1**	**2766.4**	**3338.6**	**4368.1**

Table 11.13 shows a similar approach using the end 2019 forecast. This is arguably more relevant given the analysis is being undertaken towards the end of December 2018. The consensus broker fair value price is 2944.4p for the end of 2019.

Table 11.13 Composite consensus broker valuation – end 2019 forecast

	Excellent value	Good value	Average	Poor value	Expensive
Sales	1929.8	2358.6	2948.3	3537.9	4502.8
Earnings	1932.9	2311.9	2927.8	3543.7	4699.6
Hybrid	1952.3	2335.1	2957.1	3579.2	4746.7
Average	**1938.3**	**2335.2**	**2944.4**	**3553.6**	**4649.7**

The overall broker consensus can be used to infer the margin of safety believed to be in the market by brokers. This margin is the percentage increase required in the current price to return to the overall broker consensus of fair value. (If the percentage change is negative there is currently no margin of safety.)

Example

The current share price for XP Power is 2130p. Based on the 2018 broker fair value price of 2766.4p, there is a 23% (= (1 − 2130 ÷ 2766.4)) margin of safety. Similarly, based on the 2019 broker fair value price of 2944.4p, the margin of safety widens to 27.7% (= (1 − 2130 ÷ 2944.4)). The consensus broker expectation is that there is a healthy margin of safety.

Summary

This chapter has shown how to make use of broker views on earnings and sales by translating them into a consensus view on the value of the shares using a range of approaches. The broker price ranges produced allow you to assess whether the current share price is considered fair, good value or expensive by the market (proxied by the consensus broker view) and estimate margin of safety. It also gives an idea of the potential risk to reward ratio if the shares are purchased at a certain price.

CHAPTER 12

LONG-TERM FAIR VALUE

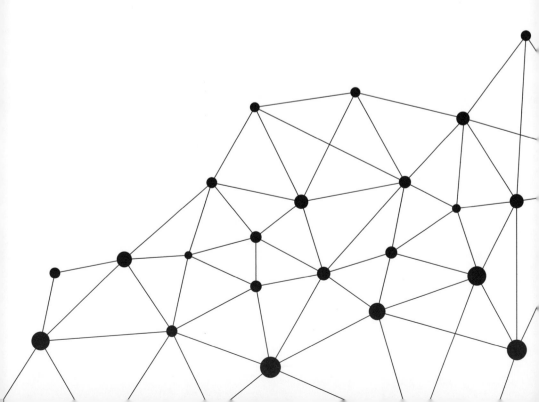

Introduction

WHILE THE PREVIOUS chapter looked at consensus broker view and the value brokers place on a company's shares over the short term (i.e., two years or less), this chapter focuses on longer term value and the likely returns from holding a company's shares over a ten-year period, or longer. You want to invest in companies that offer long-term returns with a sufficient margin of safety, as this helps to generate positive returns more consistently with less downside risk.

The methods that follow do not make use of broker forecasts, opting to use conservative growth assumptions instead. This allows you to produce an independent view on value and sense check broker forecasts.

Required investment return

The expected future long-term returns from a developed market, such as the UK or US, is typically around 7%. (This factors in a historic long-term real return of 5% and inflation averaging 2%.) Factoring in a +1% margin of safety, a basic return requirement of 8% offers a sensible starting point.

An upward adjustment to the basic return requirement can then be made to reflect how well a company has made a profit, paid a dividend and grown their revenues, profits and dividends. The more consistent the company's performance, the smaller the upward adjustment made.

The consistency score (mentioned in chapter 8) is used to measure the consistency of a company's performance. The adjusted required return is obtained by dividing the basic return of 8% by the percentage consistency score.

If a company has a perfect percentage consistency score, the required return will be the basic return of 8% (= 8% ÷ 100%). The less consistent the company, the lower the consistency score will be and the higher the required return. This is desirable as the less consistent the company is, the harder it is to forecast future performance and the larger the margin of safety required to compensate for this.

Example

XP Power has a percentage consistency score of 82% so the required return is therefore 9.8% (= 8% ÷ 82%).

A company's sensitivity to market moves is also considered when determining the required return. The more sensitive a company's share price is to overall changes in market price, the greater the return required to invest in the company, due to the increased uncertainty.

One measure of a company's market sensitivity is beta, which measures the relationship between movements in the wider market and a company's share price. If a company has a beta of 1, it indicates that the share price tends to move in line with the market. The further beta is below 1, the less sensitive the share price is to general market moves. If beta is greater than 1, the share price tends to be more volatile than the overall market.

If beta is larger than 1, the required return hurdle is obtained by multiplying the basic return requirement by beta. If beta is less than 1, the required return is equal to the basic return adjustment; if the required return hurdle is larger than the consistency adjusted return requirement, use the required return as the hurdle.

Example

XP Power has a percentage consistency score of 82% and a beta of 0.8. The adjusted return requirement is 9.8% (= 8% ÷ 82%). The required return hurdle given market volatility is 6.4% (= 8% × 0.8). This is below the adjusted return requirement, so the final return requirement is 9.8%. This is the minimum return that should be accepted for investing in XP Power.

Growth assumptions

To create a fair valuation, estimates for potential growth of sales, earnings and dividends are needed. Historic data on these three categories can be used to generate a conservative estimate of earnings, sales and dividend growth.

Using this historic data, you can also calculate the compound annual growth rate (CAGR) over five, seven and nine years. Finally, you can determine a smoothed growth rate by calculating the growth rate from the average of the oldest three years of data to the average of the newest three years.

Example

Table 12.1 shows historic earnings, dividends and sales data – XP Power.

Table 12.1 Sales, earnings and dividend data for XP Power

	2008	2009	2010	2011	2012	2013	2014	2015	2016	2017
Sales (£m)	69.3	67.3	91.8	103.6	93.9	101.1	101.1	109.7	129.8	166.8
Normalised EPS (£m)	46.4	39.3	83.2	106.4	81.3	95.1	101.1	102.8	111.2	146
DPS (p)	17.2	18.0	27.1	36.9	41.0	45.1	50.0	54.1	71.0	78.0

Table 12.2 shows the different compound growth rates for XP Power, which are calculated from the data in table 12.1.

Table 12.2 Compound annual growth rates (CAGRs) (%)

	Sales	EPS	DPS
9-year CAGR	10.3	13.6	18.3
7-year CAGR	8.9	8.4	16.3
5-year CAGR	12.2	12.4	13.7
Smoothed CAGR	8.6	11.4	18.4

From 2008 to 2017 sales have grown by 140.7% (= (166.8 ÷ 69.3) – 1), which equates to a nine-year compound annual growth rate (CAGR) of 10.3% per annum. (This is calculated using the formula $(1 + 140.7\%)^{(1/9)} - 1$) Similarly, from 2010 to 2017 sales grew by 81.7% (= (166.8 ÷ 91.8) – 1), which equates to a seven year CAGR of 8.9% (= $(1 + 81.7\%)^{(1/7)} - 1$). Sales grew by 77.6% from 2012 to 2017, which equates to 12.2% CAGR over the past five years.

From 2015 to 2017 sales averaged £135.4m (= (109.7 + 129.8 + 166.8) ÷ 3) and £76.1m (= (69.3 + 67.3 + 91.8) ÷ 3) over 2008 to 2010. The smoothed CAGR is therefore 8.6% (= $(135.4 ÷ 76.1)^{(1/7)} - 1$). The earnings and dividend growth rates are calculated in a similar way.

The long-term growth rate for sales is calculated as the lowest sales growth rate based on these four measures.

Example

Looking at table 12.2, the long-term growth rate for sales is assumed to be 8.6%, as this is the lowest growth rate of the four measures.

The broker forecast sales for XP Power are shown in table 12.3. Broker consensus expects sales to increase by 19.3% in 2018 and by 6.9% in 2019. Thus, long-term sales growth of 8.6% looks credible relative to growth over 2019.

Table 12.3 Current and forecast broker sales for XP Power

	2017	2018 (f)	2019 (f)
Sales (£m)	166.8	199.0	212.8

(f) indicates broker forecasts, taken at December 2018.

A long-term earnings growth assumption is estimated in the same way as the sales growth estimate. However, in addition to the four compound growth measures, you can also consider a sustainable growth measure: long run book value growth. This is calculated by multiplying the average retained earnings ratio by the five-year average return on equity (ROE).

The average retained earnings ratio is 1 minus the average payout ratio, which is calculated as dividends paid out over the past five years divided by normalised earnings made over the same period.

ROE figures can be found on the Morningstar website in the balance sheet summary of the finance section. You should take the average of the past five reported years ROE. The long-term growth rate for earnings is then calculated as the lowest earnings growth rate based on the five measures.

Example

Looking at table 12.1, XP Power has earned 556.2p of EPS and paid out 298.2p of DPS over the past five years. The payout ratio is therefore 53.6% (= 298.2 ÷ 556.2), which means that the average retained earnings ratio is 46.4%.

Table 12.4 Return on equity for XP Power

	2008	2009	2010	2011	2012	2013	2014	2015	2016	2017
ROE (%)	30.1	25.3	43.8	41.3	26.6	27.9	26.0	23.4	21.9	25.5

Table 12.4 shows the return on equity (ROE) earned by XP Power over the past decade. The average return on equity over the past five years is 24.9% (= (27.9% + 26.0% + 23.4% + 21.9% + 25.5%) ÷ 5). The sustainable growth rate is therefore 11.6% (= 46.4% × 24.9%).

Looking at table 12.2 you can see that the lowest EPS growth rate of the four measures is 8.4%. This is less than the sustainable growth rate of 11.6% and the smoothed earnings CAGR of 11.4%. The long-term growth rate is therefore put at 8.4%, which is in line with sales growth of 8.6%. (Note that earnings tend to be more volatile than sales and an alternative approach is to use the lower of the smoothed earnings CAGR, the sustainable growth rate and the sales growth rate when in doubt.)

The current and broker forecast earnings are shown in table 12.5. Earnings are expected to grow by 20.6% in 2018 and 7.7% in 2019. The long-term earnings growth of 8.4% is above earnings growth in 2019, but is not too far out to consider an adjustment.

Table 12.5 Current and broker forecast earnings for XP Power

	2017	2018 (f)	2019 (f)
Normalised EPS (p)	146.0	176.0	189.5

(f) indicates broker forecasts, taken at December 2018.

The long-term growth rate for dividends is calculated as the lowest dividend growth rate based on the four compound measures. The compound growth rate may not exceed the assumed long-term earnings growth rate. If the lowest rate is negative, set the growth rate to zero or the lowest positive number, depending on your qualitative view about future performance.

Example

Looking at table 12.2, the lowest CAGR for dividends is 13.7% over five years. This is above the long-term earnings growth rate of 8.4%. The long-term dividend growth rate is therefore lowered to 8.4%.

Table 12.6 Current and broker forecast dividends for XP Power

	2017	2018 (f)	2019 (f)
Dividend per share (p)	78.0	82.5	87.5

(f) indicates broker forecasts, taken at December 2018.

The current dividends per share and the next two years of broker forecasts are shown in table 12.6. Dividends are expected to grow by 5.7% over 2018 and by 6.1% over 2019. This equates to a CAGR of 5.9% over 2018 and 2019. This is 2.5% lower than the proposed long-term dividend growth rate.

If dividends grow in line with broker expectations over the first two years and then by 8.4% over the next three years, this implies a compound growth rate of 7.9% (= $((1 + 5.9\%)^2 \times (1 + 8.4\%)^8)^{(1/10)}$) per annum over the next ten years. To be prudent, the long-term dividend growth rate is set at 7.9%.

Table 12.7 Summary of long-term growth assumptions

	Growth
Sales (£m)	8.6%
Normalised EPS (£m)	8.4%
DPS (p)	7.9%
NAV ps (p)	11.6%

Table 12.7 summarises the long-term growth assumptions for XP Power. The last line shows the long run book value (or net asset value) growth, which was calculated earlier.

Earnings yield

Earnings yield is a quick way to assess the potential return on capital (i.e., equity and debt) invested in the company. It is defined as earnings before interest and tax (EBIT) divided by the enterprise value. EBIT is a measure of profit that is not dependent on tax regulations or the capital structure, as it doesn't include interest expenses. Enterprise value (EV) equals the value of the operations of the company attributable to all providers of capital. EV is not dependent on the choice of capital structure as it incorporates all debt and equity. We therefore don't have to consider the percentage invested in debt and equity with this measure.

The Morningstar stock report provides the latest reported values for EBIT and EBITDA (which also excludes depreciation and amortisation) as well as forecasts for the next two years. Enterprise value is not directly quoted, but the EV/EBITDA ratio is stated, which allows EV to be backed out quickly. One can then use the EBIT forecasts and current EV to gain insight into future earnings yield.

Example

Consider table 12.8, which shows EBIT, EBITDA and EV/EBITDA for XP Power.

Towards the end of December 2018, the current EV/EBITDA ratio is 11.8 and EBITDA is £38.6m. The EV is therefore £454.3m (= 11.77 × £38.6m). EBIT at the end of 2017 is £32.4m, which implies an earnings yield of 7.1% (= 32.4 ÷ 454.3). EBIT is forecast to rise to £42.8m in 2018 and £46.7m in 2019.

This means that earnings yield is expected to rise to 9.4% in 2018 and 10.3% in 2019, assuming the enterprise value remains the same. The expected earnings yield over 2019 is currently above the total return requirement of 9.8%. This suggests that, given the assumptions made, XP Power is capable of achieving the required returns.

Table 12.8 EBIT, EBITDA and EV/EBITDA for XP Power

	2017	2018 (f)	2019 (f)
EBIT (£m)	32.4	42.8	46.7
EBITDA (£m)	38.6	49.2	54.1
EV/EBITDA	11.77	9.2	8.4
Earnings yield (%)	7.1	9.4	10.3

(f) indicates broker forecasts, taken at December 2018.

Asset-based fair valuation

The growth in assets can be used to assess the likely returns from an investment in a company. This valuation method is ideal for financial companies, such as banks and insurance companies, which can easily manipulate earnings and where underlying asset value is arguably more important. Companies that have large amounts of assets on their balance sheet, such as property and utility companies, may also be better valued using this method too. Conversely, companies with low amounts of physical assets, such as technology companies, should avoid using this valuation methodology as it is not suitable.

The asset-based fair valuation method typically offers a more conservative valuation than other methods described in this chapter. The steps in this asset-return-based calculation are as follows:

Step 1: Estimate the net tangible asset value per share (NAV ps) in ten years' time

The current tangible asset value per share can be found in the Morningstar report, and is usually referred to as net tangible asset value per share (NAV ps).

To estimate the NAV ps in ten years' time, it is assumed that assets grow in line with the long-term assumption. Therefore, it is calculated by multiplying the current asset value per share by 1 plus the asset growth rate, to the power of ten.

Example

XP Power has NAV ps of 272.7p at the end of 2017. The long-term asset value growth rate is 11.6%. NAV ps in ten years' time is therefore going to be 817.2p (= 1.116^{10} × 272.7p = 2.997 × 272.7p).

Step 2: Estimate the earnings per share in ten years' time

The earnings per share in ten years' time is obtained by multiplying the NAV ps in ten years' time by the average return on equity.

Example

The average return on equity was previously calculated to be 24.9%. The EPS in ten years' time is therefore 203.5p (= 24.9% × 817.2p). A sense check against historic EPS shows that this EPS number looks plausible.

Step 3: Estimate the central price in ten years' time

Chapter 11 showed how to calculate the average price to earnings, the average low price to earnings and the average high price to earnings ratios over the past five years. The central price in ten years' time is calculated by multiplying the average price to earnings by the estimate of earnings in ten years' time.

Example

Table 12.9 summarises the average PE statistics for XP Power, which were calculated in the previous chapter. The central estimate of the share price in ten years' time is 3154.3p (= 15.5 × 203.5p).

Table 12.9 PE ratio summary statistics

	Low	Average low	Average	Average high	High
PE Ratio (p)	10.2	12.2	15.5	18.7	24.8

Step 4: Estimate a price range for the share price in ten years' time

The low price in ten years' time is calculated by multiplying the average low PE ratio by the estimate of earnings in ten years' time. The high price in ten years' time is calculated by multiplying the average high price to earnings ratio by the estimate of earnings in ten years' time. This provides a plausible range for the share price in ten years' time.

Example

For XP Power, the low price in ten years' time is 2482.7p (= 12.2 × 203.5p), and the high price in ten years' time is 3805.5p (= 18.7 × 203.5p). Thus, we expect the price in ten years' time to be in the range of 2482.7p and 3805.5p, provided company valuations are not at extreme levels.

Step 5: Estimate the dividends paid over the next ten years

To estimate the amount of dividends payable over the next ten years, you first need to work out the total amount of earnings that will be earned over the next ten years. To do this, assume that net asset value grows in line with our long-term assumption each year. Assuming the return on equity is in line with the average return on equity, the EPS in each year will be the average return on equity multiplied by the net asset value in that year. Using this approach, you can calculate the EPS paid out over the next ten years.

Example

The NAV ps at the end of 2017 is 272.7p and the long-term asset value growth rate is 11.6%. The NAV ps in one years' time is 304.3p (= 1.116 × 817.2p). The following years' net asset value is 339.6p (= 1.116 × 304.3p). Continuing with this calculation you can estimate the NAV ps over the next ten years, as shown in table 12.10.

Table 12.10 Future net asset value and earnings per share

	Year 1	Year 2	Year 3	Year 4	Year 5	Year 6	Year 7	Year 8	Year 9	Year 10
NAV ps (p)	304.3	339.6	379.0	423.0	472.1	526.8	587.9	656.1	732.3	817.2
EPS (p)	75.8	84.6	94.4	105.3	117.5	131.2	146.4	163.4	182.3	203.5

Multiplying the estimated future net asset value numbers by 24.9% (our choice of return on equity) you obtain the estimated future EPS over each of the next ten years. The estimated future EPS are shown in the second row of table 12.10. Total EPS over the next ten years is 1304.4p.

Note that the EPS numbers in the first few years look low compared to the EPS history and broker forecasts over 2018 and 2019. This suggests that this valuation method may be less applicable than others.

The percentage of earnings paid out as dividends is assumed to be in line with the average rate paid out over the last five years. The total dividends paid out over the next ten years is estimated by multiplying the total earnings earned over the next ten years multiplied by the average payout ratio.

Example

The payout ratio was previously calculated as 53.6%. The total dividends paid out over the next ten years is therefore estimated to be 699.2p (= 0.536 × 1304.4p).

Step 6: Estimate the potential return at the current share price

The overall share price in ten years' time is the central share price in ten years' time plus the total dividends paid out over the next ten years. The annualised expected return is the CAGR of the share price over the next ten years. If the expected return is above the required return the shares may be purchased, provided the company shares are on the buy list and the rules about portfolio allocation are followed.

Example

The overall share price in ten years' time including the dividends paid out over the next ten years is 3853.5p (= 3154.3p + 699.2p). If the current price is 2130p, the annualised total return is expected to be 6.1% (= (3853.3 ÷ 2130)$^{(1/10)}$ – 1). This is below the required return of 9.8% and implies that you should wait for a better price to invest.

A more conservative estimate of the likely returns can be obtained by using an estimate of the share price in ten years' time that is consistent with the lower end of the valuation spectrum.

Example

The conservative estimate of the share price in ten years' time is 3181.9p (= 2482.7p + 699.2p). The annualised total return is then expected to be 4.1% (= (3181.9 ÷ 2130)$^{(1/10)}$ – 1). This is well below the required return of 10%, meaning you should wait for a better price before investing.

A higher, more optimistic estimate of the likely returns can be obtained by using a high estimate of the share price in ten years' time. If the optimistic return estimate is below the required return, the shares offer poor value and should not be purchased until the price has fallen sufficiently.

Example

The optimistic estimate of the share price in ten years' time is 4504.7p (= 3805.5p + 699.2p). The annualised total return is expected to be 7.8% (= (4504.7 ÷ 2130)$^{(1/10)}$ – 1). This is still well below the required return of 9.8% and implies that the shares are potentially poor value.

Step 7: Produce a sticker price for the company

The sticker price is the maximum price you should pay for the company's shares. It is obtained by discounting the overall share price in ten years' time including the dividends paid by the required return.

Example

The overall share price in ten years' time, including the dividends paid out over the next ten years, is 3853.5p and the required return is 9.8%. The sticker price is therefore 1513p (= $3853.5 \div 1.098^{10}$), well below the current price of 2130p. Given the assumptions made, this is the price that will deliver the required return.

Earnings-based fair valuation

This methodology uses growth in earnings to estimate the potential return from investing in a company's shares. Earnings are an effective proxy for the issues driving price, volume and costs. The performance of these variables helps determine the success of the company and the share price.

This methodology cannot be used for companies with no earnings. If earnings are very low or negative, use of the PE ratio is inappropriate. If earnings are very low but positive, the PE ratio will be so high that it is not meaningful. If earnings are negative, future earnings cannot be easily projected forward and the PE ratio is negative. Companies that tend to suffer from this problem are either highly cyclical companies, which suffer from periods of low earnings or losses at the bottom of an economic cycle, or start-up companies that are yet to make a profit. Fortunately, our screening approach will typically eliminate these types of company from consideration.

Equally, the earnings valuation method should not be used for financial companies, such as insurance, banks or property. These companies are normally valued on assets rather than earnings.

The steps in the earnings-based fair valuation calculation are as follows:

Step 1: Estimate earnings per share in ten years' time

To estimate the EPS in ten years' time, we assume that earnings grow in line with our long-term assumption. EPS in ten years' time is calculated by multiplying the current EPS by 1 plus the earnings growth rate to the power of ten.

Example

XP Power has current earnings per share of 146p in 2017. The long-term earnings growth rate is 8.4%. Earnings per share in ten years' time is therefore going to be 327.1p (= $1.084^{10} \times 146p$).

Step 2: Estimate the central price in ten years' time

The central price in ten years' time is calculated by multiplying the average PE by the estimate of earnings in ten years' time.

Example

Table 12.9 summarises the average PE statistics for XP Power, which were calculated in the previous chapter. The central estimate of the share price in ten years' time is 5070p (= 15.5 × 327.1p).

Step 3: Estimate a price range for the share price in ten years' time

The low price in ten years' time is calculated by multiplying the average low PE ratio by the estimate of earnings in ten years' time. The high price in ten years' time is calculated by multiplying the average high PE ratio by the estimate of earnings in ten years' time. This provides a plausible range for the share price in ten years' time.

Example

For XP Power, the low price in ten years' time is 3990.6p (= 12.2 × 327.1p), and the high price in ten years' time is 6116.8p (= 18.7 × 327.1p). Thus, the price in ten years' time is expected to be in the range of 3990.6p to 6116.8p, provided company valuations are not at extreme levels.

Step 4: Estimate the dividends paid over the next ten years

To estimate the amount of dividends payable over the next ten years you need to work out the total amount of earnings that will be earned over this period. The EPS in a year can be obtained by multiplying EPS in the previous year by 1 plus the long-term earnings growth assumption. This allows you to calculate EPS over the next ten years and sum them together to obtain the expected total EPS earned over the next ten years.

Example

The current EPS is 146p per share and the long-term earnings growth rate is 8.4%. The earnings per share in one years' time is 158.3p (= 1.084 × 146p). The following years' earnings per share is 171.6p (= 1.084 × 158.3p). Continuing with this calculation you can estimate the EPS over the next ten years, as shown in table 12.11.

Table 12.11 Future earnings per share

	Year 1	Year 2	Year 3	Year 4	Year 5	Year 6	Year 7	Year 8	Year 9	Year 10
EPS (p)	158.3	171.6	186.0	201.6	218.5	236.9	256.8	278.3	301.7	327.1

The total dividends paid out over the next ten years is estimated by multiplying the total earnings over the period by the average payout ratio.

Example

From table 12.11, total earnings are estimated to be 2336.7p per share over the next ten years. The payout ratio was previously calculated as 53.6%. The total dividends paid out over the next ten years is therefore estimated to be 1252.5p (= 0.536 × 2336.7p).

Step 5: Estimate the potential return at the current share price

The share price in ten years' time including the dividends paid out is the central share price plus the sum of the dividends paid out over the next ten years. The annualised expected return is the CAGR of the share price over the next ten years. If the expected return is above the required return, the shares may be purchased.

Example

The central estimate of the share price in ten years' time is 5070p. The overall share price in ten years' time including the dividends paid out is 6322.5p (= 5070p + 1252.5p). If the current price of XP Power is 2130p, the annualised total return is expected to be 11.5% (= (6322.5 ÷ 2130) $^{(1/10)}$ − 1). This is above the required return of 9.8% and implies that the shares are cheap enough to invest in.

A more conservative estimate of the likely returns can be obtained by using a low estimate of the share price in ten years' time. If this is above the required return, the shares are attractively priced and likely to offer excellent value.

Example

The conservative estimate of the share price in ten years' time is 3990.6p. A conservative share price in ten years' time, including the dividends paid out over the next ten years is 5243.1p (= 3990.6p + 1252.5p). If the current price of XP Power is 2130p, the annualised total return is then expected to be 9.4% (= $(5243.1 \div 2130)^{(1/10)} - 1$). This is below the required return of 9.8%, which implies that there may not be enough margin of safety when valuations are based on earnings.

A more optimistic estimate of the likely returns can be obtained by using a high estimate of the share price in ten years' time. If the optimistic return estimate is below the required return the shares are likely to offer poor value.

Example

The optimistic estimate of the share price in ten years' time is 6116.8p. The overall share price in ten years' time including the dividends paid out over the next ten years is 7369.3p (= 6116.8p + 1252.5p). If the current price of XP Power is 2130p, the annualised total return is expected to be 13.2% (= $(7369.3 \div 2130)^{(1/10)} - 1$). This is well above the required return of 13.2% and implies that the shares have good upside. Returns are expected to range between 9.4% and 13.2%.

Step 6: Produce a sticker price for the company

The sticker price is the maximum price we currently want to pay for the company's shares. It is obtained by discounting the expected overall share price in ten years' time including the dividends paid by the required return.

Example

The overall share price in ten years' time, including the dividends paid is 6322.5p and the required return is 9.8%. The sticker price is therefore 2482.4p (= $6322.5p \div 1.098^{10}$). Given the assumptions made, this is the highest price that will deliver the required return. This suggests the current price of 2130p provides a 14.2% (= $(2482.4 - 2130) \div 2482.4$) margin of safety.

Sales-based fair valuation

This method uses growth in sales to estimate the potential return from investing in a company's shares. Sales can be a more reliable indicator of growth as figures are harder to manipulate than earnings.

This sales-based method can be used to double check that a company's growth has not become overvalued. Equally, it is useful for evaluating recovery situations. For example, if a company begins to suffer losses and, as a result, has no earnings (and no meaningful PE ratio) to assess likely returns, the sales figures can be used instead as these tend to be more stable than earnings. The ratio is less appropriate for service companies like banks or insurers that don't really have sales.

The steps in the sales-based fair valuation are as follows:

Step 1: Estimate sales per share in ten years' time

SPS is calculated by dividing total sales by the total number of shares outstanding. Assuming sales growth is in line with the long-term growth assumption, SPS in ten years' time is calculated by multiplying the latest SPS by 1 plus the sales growth rate to the power of 10.

Example

In 2017, XP Power reported an SPS of 860.3p. The long-term sales growth rate is 8.6%. SPS in ten years' time is therefore expected to be 1963.1p (= $1.086^{10} \times 860.3p$).

Step 2: Estimate the central price in ten years' time

The previous chapter showed how to calculate the average price to sales ratio as well as the average low and average high price to sales ratios over the past five years. The central price in ten years' time is calculated by multiplying the average price to sales by the estimate of sales in ten years' time.

Example

Table 12.12 summarises the average PSR statistics for XP Power which were calculated in the previous chapter. The central estimate of the share price in ten years' time is 5398.5p (= 2.75 × 1963.1p).

Table 12.12 Price to sales ratio summary statistics for XP Power

	Low	Average low	Average	Average high	High
Price to sales ratio (PSR)	1.8	2.2	2.75	3.3	4.2

Step 3: Estimate a price range for the share price in ten years' time

The low price in ten years' time is calculated by multiplying the average low price to sales ratio by the estimate of sales in ten years' time. Similarly, the high price in ten years' time is calculated by multiplying the average high price to sales ratio by the estimate of sales in ten years' time. This provides a plausible range for the share price in ten years' time.

Example

For XP Power, the low price in ten years' time is 4318.8p ($= 2.2 \times 1963.1$p), and the high price is 6478.2p ($= 3.3 \times 1963.1$p). Thus, we expect the price in ten years' time to be in the range of 4318.8p to 6478.2p, provided company valuations are not at extreme levels.

Step 4: Estimate the dividends paid over the next ten years

To estimate the amount of dividends payable over the next ten years you need to work out the total amount of earnings that will be earned over the period. To do this, assume that sales grow in line with the long-term assumption.

Example

The SPS in 2017 is 860.3p per share and the long-term sales growth rate is 8.6%. The SPS in one year's time is 934.3p ($= 1.086 \times 860.3$p). The following year's SPS is 1014.6p ($= 1.086 \times 934.3$p). Continuing with this calculation you can estimate the SPS over the next ten years, as shown in the top row of numbers in table 12.13.

Table 12.13 Future sales per share and earnings per share

	Year 1	Year 2	Year 3	Year 4	Year 5	Year 6	Year 7	Year 8	Year 9	Year 10
SPS (p)	934.3	1014.6	1101.9	1196.7	1299.6	1411.3	1532.7	1664.5	1807.7	1963.1
EPS (p)	165.4	179.6	195.0	211.8	230.0	249.8	271.3	294.6	320.0	347.5

The profit margin is the proportion of sales converted into earnings. The average profit margin is defined as the average price to sales ratio divided by the average price to earnings ratio.

Example

From table 12.12, the average PSR for XP Power is 2.75 and, from table 12.9, its average PE ratio is 15.5. Thus, the average profit margin is 17.7% (= 2.75 ÷ 15.5).

Assuming the profit margin is in line with the average, the EPS in a particular year will be the average profit margin multiplied by the SPS in that year. You can calculate the EPS over the next ten years and sum them together to obtain the expected total EPS earned over the next ten years.

Example

Multiplying the estimated future SPS numbers by 17.7% (the average profit margin) you obtain the estimated future EPS over each of the next ten years. The estimated future EPS are shown in the second row of table 12.13, from which total earnings over the next ten years can be estimated to be 2465p per share.

The total dividends paid out over the next ten years is estimated by multiplying the total earnings over the period by the average payout ratio.

Example

The average payout ratio for XP Power is 53.6%. Thus, the total dividends paid out over the next ten years is estimated to be 1321.2p (= 0.536 × 2465p).

Step 5: Estimate the potential return at the current share price

The overall share price in ten years' time, including the dividends paid out, is the central share price plus the total dividends paid out over ten years. The annualised expected return is the CAGR of the share price over the next ten years. If the central expected return is above the required return the shares may be purchased.

Example

The central estimate of the share price in ten years' time is 5398.5p. The overall share price in ten years' time including the dividends paid out over the next ten years is 6719.7p (= 5398.5p + 1321.2p). If the current price of XP Power is 2130p, the annualised total return is expected to be 12.2% (= $(6719.7 \div 2130)^{(1/10)} - 1$). This is above the required return of 9.8% and means that an investment in XP Power is likely to yield more than the required return.

A more conservative estimate of the likely returns can be obtained by using a low estimate of the share price in ten years' time. If the conservative return estimate is above the required return, the shares are attractively priced and are likely to offer good value.

Example

The low estimate of the share price in ten years' time is 4318.8p. A conservative share price in ten years' time, including the dividends paid out over the next ten years, is 5640p (= 4318.8p + 1321.2p). If the current price is 2130p, the annualised total return is then expected to be 10.2% (= $(5640 \div 2130)^{(1/10)} - 1$).

A more optimistic estimate of the likely returns can be obtained by using a high estimate of the share price in ten years' time. If the optimistic return estimate is below the required return, the shares are expensive and should not be purchased until the share price has fallen sufficiently.

Example

The optimistic estimate of the share price in ten years' time is 6478.2p. The overall share price in ten years' time, including the dividends paid out over the next ten years, is 7799.4p (= 6478.2p + 1321.2p). If the current price is 2130p, the annualised total return is expected to be 13.9% (= $(7799.4 \div 2130)^{(1/10)} - 1$). This is above the required return of 9.8%, which suggests the shares have plenty of upside. Based on sales, the shares are expected to return between 10.2% and 13.9%.

Step 6: Produce a sticker price for the company.

The sticker price is the maximum price you should pay for the company's shares. It is obtained by discounting the overall share price in ten years' time including the dividends paid by the required return.

Example

The overall share price in ten years' time, including the dividends paid out over the next ten years, is 6719.7p and the required return is 9.8%. The sticker price is therefore 2638.3p (= 6719.7p ÷ 1.098^{10}). Given the assumptions made, this is the highest price that will deliver the desired required return. The current price of 2130p is well below the sticker price of 2638.3p and currently offers a margin of safety of 19.3% (= (2638.3 – 2130) ÷ 2638.3).

Quick and easy dividend-based fair valuation

This valuation method can be used to place a value on large income or value companies that consistently pay out a dividend every year. It cannot be used to value companies that do not pay a dividend or young companies that irregularly pay a dividend, which typically rules out growth companies.

The simple approach outlined here produces a fair value price but does not provide an estimate of the likely return over the next ten years. However, it benefits from being a quick way to estimate the sticker price.

The steps in the dividend-based fair valuation calculation are as follows:

Step 1: Calculate the excess return over dividend growth required

The excess return required over the dividend growth is calculated by subtracting the long-term growth rate from the required return.

Example

The required return for XP Power is 9.8% and the long-term dividend growth rate is 7.9%. The excess return required over the dividend growth is therefore 1.9% (= 9.8% – 7.9%).

Step 2: Estimate the central price

The central price is determined by dividing the current dividend by the excess return required over the dividend growth.

Example

The 2017 dividend for XP Power is 78p. The central price is therefore 4105.3p (= 78p ÷ 1.9%). This is well above the current price of 2130p and suggests there is a 72.5% (= (4105.3 – 2130) ÷ 4105.3) margin of safety.

Step 3: Determine the fair value price range

The price range is determined by varying the dividend growth rate. The lower end of the price range is calculated by reducing the long-term dividend growth rate by 25% and repeating the calculations in steps 1 and 2. Similarly, the upper price range is determined by raising the long-term dividend growth rate by 25%; if this growth rate is above the required return, simply use the central projection as the upper bound.

Example

The lower dividend growth rate is 5.9% (= 0.75 × 7.9%) and the upper growth range is 9.9% (= 1.25 × 7.9%). The lower end of the price range is 2000p (= 78p ÷ (9.8% – 5.9%)) and the upper end of the price range is set at the central price of 4105.3p. Thus, the fair value price range is 2000p to 4105.3p. The current share price is 2130p, which suggests there is more upside than downside.

Dividend-based fair valuation

This valuation method can be used to place a value on large income or value companies that consistently pay out a dividend every year. It cannot be used to value companies that irregularly pay a dividend or do not pay a dividend. Unlike the quick and easy version, this approach produces likely return ranges as well as a sticker price.

The steps in the dividend-based fair valuation calculation are as follows:

Step 1: Determine the historic dividend yield range

The dividend yield for a company is the DPS divided by the share price. The dividend-based share price range is obtained by looking at the share price the company traded at during a given year. The highest and lowest dividend yield is calculated by dividing the share price by the share price low/high in the same accounting year.

The average high/low dividend yield is calculated by averaging the high or low dividend yields achieved over the past five years. An overall average dividend yield is obtained by averaging the high and low average dividend yields.

Example

Table 12.14 shows the historic DPS paid out each accounting year and the share price range for XP Power. This information is used to calculate the highest and lowest dividend yield attained each year. For example, in 2017 the highest dividend yield was 4.5% (= 78 ÷ 1725) and the lowest dividend yield was 2.2% (= 78 ÷ 3626.4).

Table 12.14 Historic dividend yield ranges for XP Power

	2013	2014	2015	2016	2017	Average
High Price (p)	1630.0	1798.0	1750.0	1845.1	3626.4	
Low Price (p)	972.3	1340.0	1375.0	1396.8	1725.0	
DPS (p)	45.1	50.0	54.1	71.0	78.0	
Dividend yield – high (%)	4.6	3.7	3.9	5.1	4.5	4.4
Dividend yield – low (%)	2.8	2.8	3.1	3.8	2.2	2.9

The high dividend yields averaged 4.4%, while the low dividend yields averaged 2.9%. The overall average dividend yield is 3.7% (= (4.4% + 2.9%) ÷ 2).

Step 2: Estimate the dividend per share paid out in year ten

To estimate the DPS in ten years' time, it is assumed that dividends grow in line with the long-term dividend growth assumption. The DPS in ten years' time is calculated by multiplying the current DPS by 1 plus the dividend growth rate to the power of 10.

Example

The current dividend per share is 78p and the long-term dividend growth rate is 7.9%. The dividend in ten years' time is therefore estimated to be 166.8p (= 78p × 1.079^{10}).

Step 3: Estimate the central price in ten years' time

The central price in ten years' time is calculated by dividing the DPS in ten years' time by the average dividend yield.

Example

The average dividend yield over the past five years was 3.7%. The central price for XP Power is therefore 4508.1p (= 166.8p ÷ 0.037).

Step 4: Estimate a price range for the share price in ten years' time

The low/high price in ten years' time is calculated by dividing the DPS in ten years' time by the average high/low dividend yield. This provides a plausible range for the share price in ten years' time.

Example

The average high and low dividend yield are 4.4% and 2.9%, respectively. The low price is therefore 3790.9p (= 166.8p ÷ 0.044) and the high price is 5751.7p (= 166.8p ÷ 0.029).

Step 5: Estimate the dividends paid over the next ten years

The amount of dividends per share (DPS) paid out each year can be estimated using the current dividend and the estimate of long-term dividend growth. The estimate of DPS in one year's time is the current dividend multiplied by 1 plus the growth rate. The DPS in two years' time is the estimate of DPS in year one multiplied by 1 plus the growth rate. This approach can be extended to estimate the DPS paid out over the next ten years.

Example

The current dividend of XP Power is 78p and long-term dividend growth is 7.9%. The dividend paid out in the following year is therefore 84.2p (= 78p × 1.079) and in year two is 90.8p (= 84.2p × 1.079). The dividends paid out over the following years are similarly calculated and shown in table 12.15. The total dividends paid out over the next ten years is 1213.4p.

Table 12.15 Future dividends per share

	Year 1	Year 2	Year 3	Year 4	Year 5	Year 6	Year 7	Year 8	Year 9	Year 10
DPS (p)	84.2	90.8	98.0	105.7	114.1	123.1	132.8	143.3	154.6	166.8

Step 6: Estimate the potential return at the current share price

The overall share price in ten years' time including the dividends paid out is the central share price plus the total dividends paid out over ten years. The annualised expected return is the CAGR of the share price over the next ten years. If the central expected return is above the required return, the shares may be purchased.

Example

The central share price in ten years' time is 4508.1p and the total dividends paid out is 1213.4p. The overall share price is therefore 5721.5p (= 4508.1p + 1213.4p). The current share price is 2130p and the estimated CAGR is therefore 10.4% (= $(5721.5 \div 2130)^{(1/10)} - 1$). This is above the required return of 9.8%.

A more conservative estimate of the likely returns can be obtained by using the share price low.

Example

The low share price in ten years' time is 3790.9p and the total dividends paid out is 1213.4p. The overall low share price is therefore 5004.3p (= 3790.9p + 1213.4p). Thus the CAGR is 8.9% (= $(5004.3 \div 2130)^{(1/10)} - 1$).

A more optimistic estimate of the likely returns can be obtained by using a higher share price in ten years' time.

Example

The high share price in ten years' time is 5751.7p and the total dividends paid out is 1213.4p. The overall high share price is therefore 6965.1p (= 5751.7p + 1213.4p). Thus, the CAGR is 12.6% (= (6965.1 ÷ 2130) $^{(1/10)}$ − 1) and returns are expected to range between 8.9% and 12.6%. This again suggests there is more upside than downside when compared against the required return of 9.8%.

Step 7: Produce a sticker price for the company.

The sticker price is obtained by discounting the overall share price in ten years' time by the required annual return.

Example

The overall share price in ten years' time is 5721.5p and the required annual return is 9.8%. The sticker price is therefore 2246.4p (= 5721.5p ÷ 1.098^{10}). Thus, the current share price of 2130p has a 5.2% (= (2246.4 − 2130) ÷ 2246.4) margin of safety.

Overall fair valuation

The different valuation methods based on assets, earnings, sales and dividends produce different estimates for the expected investment return and sticker price. You will generally want to see at least two of the methods indicating that the current share price offers value.

For companies where the valuation methods are equally applicable you will need to combine the valuation methods to produce an overall fair valuation, which gives a composite expected long-term return and a sticker price.

One option is to take an average of the valuation methods that are applicable to a company. Alternatively, a more pragmatic approach is to select the valuation method that has the closest sticker price to the current share price.

Example

Table 12.16 summarises the estimated long-term returns from investing in XP Power and the sticker price under each valuation method.

Table 12.16 Estimated long-term returns

Valuation method	Expected return (%)			Sticker Price (p)
	Low	Average	High	
Earnings yield	-	7.1	-	-
Asset	4.1	6.1	7.8	1513.0
Earnings	9.4	11.5	13.2	2482.4
Sales	10.2	12.2	13.9	2638.3
Dividends	8.9	10.4	12.6	2246.4
Overall	**8.9**	**10.4**	**12.6**	**2246.4**

The asset valuation method suggests that XP Power is expensive. However, this approach generates low earnings projections relative to recent history, and is not as credible as other methods for XP Power. In addition, XP Power is not an asset-heavy company, making this method less relevant.

The earnings, sales and dividend methods all indicate that an investment in XP Power at a share price of 2130p will likely deliver the required return of 9.8%; the average returns are all above 9.8% and the share price is less than the proposed sticker prices. The earnings and dividend methods have estimated lower bound returns that are below the required return, which suggest that weak valuations risk the required return not being achieved over the long term.

The dividend valuation method produces a fair valuation method that is closest to the current share price. It suggests that an investment in XP Power will offer a return of between 8.9% and 12.6%, with an expected return of 10.4%.

Summary

This chapter has shown you how to work out the required return for a company and how to value its shares using a variety of different approaches. These methods help you to assess the possible returns that might be generated from an investment in company shares at their current price. Using this knowledge, you can then make an informed decision about whether it is currently worthwhile investing in companies on the buy list.

CHAPTER 13

CHARTING FOR
INVESTORS

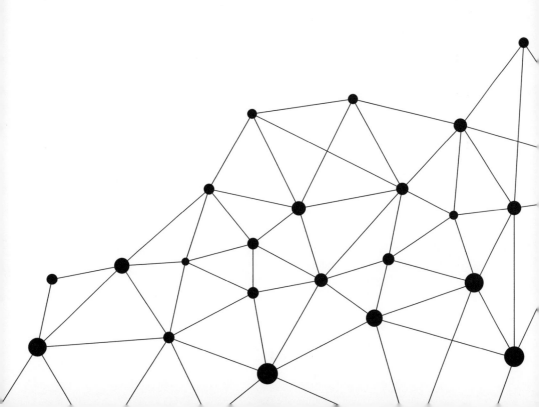

Introduction

CHARTS AND TECHNICAL analysis can be used to better understand what the current price trends are for the markets and companies you are interested in. They also provide a feel for overall sentiment, which can help decide whether to favour growth or value companies.

Such insight will help you to avoid investing in companies during periods of bearish sentiment, where companies' share prices tend to fall together. Moreover, when sentiment is bearish, waiting until downward price pressure abates may give you a better purchase price for the company's shares as well as afford some time to check your analysis and underlying assumptions.

Conversely, bullish company sentiment and no obvious areas of price resistance shows that investors have noticed the disparity to underlying value and that any investment in the company will be supported by positive price momentum. This is a good time to invest or add to positions in the company.

> Colour versions of charts are available at www.theequityedge.com and are also included in the eBook version, which every purchaser of a physical copy of the book can download for free from ebooks.harriman-house. com/equityedge. Links to the original colour charts are included under the relevant figures.

Weekly chart set-up

To identify the medium-term price trend weekly price charts are used. Weekly charts tend to smooth out the day-to-day volatility, cutting out much of the noise that is found in the daily chart. This makes it easier to identify underlying trends and key areas of support and resistance.

Candlestick charts

Weekly candlestick charts are used to help identify the underlying trend. Each candlestick in the chart represents the range of prices the shares traded at over the week. The body of each candlestick shows the area between the open and close of the week, while the area between the high and low of the candlestick shows the overall price range. The shadows of a candlestick show where price traded outside of the open and close price range.

Figure 13.1 Structure of candlesticks

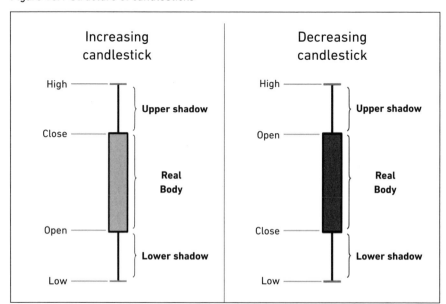

www.theequityedge.com/wp-content/uploads/2020/02/Figure-13.1.png

The structure of candlesticks is summarised in figure 13.1. An increasing candlestick is green (shown as light grey in black and white versions of the book) to demonstrate that the weekly price closed above the opening price and moved higher across the week. Conversely, a decreasing candlestick is red, (shown as dark grey in black and white versions of the book) indicating that the weekly price closed below the opening price of the week.

Figure 13.2 shows a weekly chart of the FTSE 100 from the Trading View website (tradingview.com). The lines on the chart represent different (exponential) moving averages of the closing prices.

Figure 13.2 Weekly chart of FTSE 100

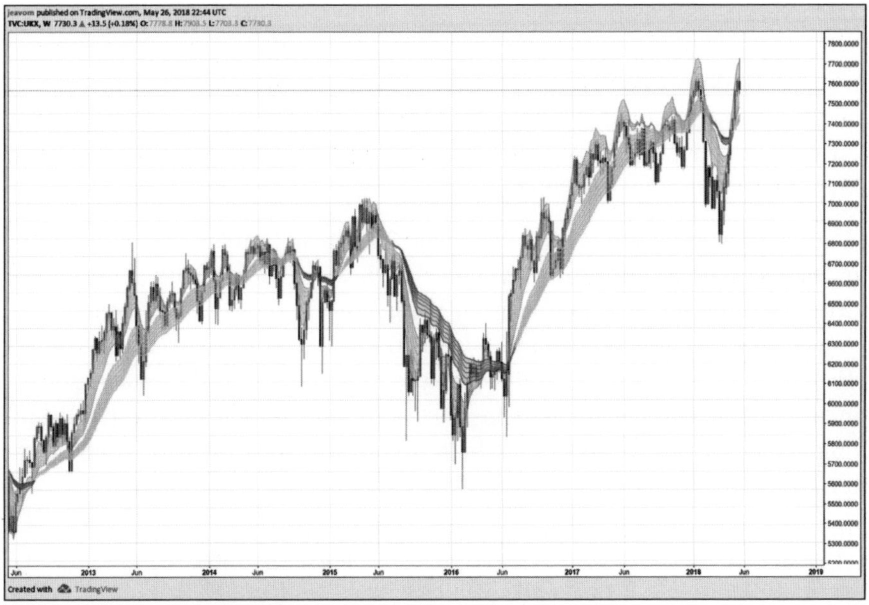

Source: Trading View (tradingview.com)

www.theequityedge.com/wp-content/uploads/2020/02/Figure-13.2.png

Moving averages

Weekly moving averages are used to help identify price trends. Each moving average calculates the (exponentially) weighted average price over a specified moving period. For example, a 21-week moving average will calculate the average price over each period consisting of 21 consecutive weeks' closing prices.

Each weekly chart has two groups of moving averages: a short-term group representing the traders in the market and a long-term group representing the more conservative, longer term investors. The trader group consists of the three-, five-, seven-, nine-, 11- and 13-week moving averages, while the investor group consists of the 21-, 24-, 27-, 30-, 33- and 36-week moving averages.

The ribbons of moving averages for these two groups are used to filter out the short-term price movements while highlighting the underlying price trend.

Defining a weekly price trend

Weekly price trends and their strength are determined by the direction and relative position of two groups of moving averages. This technique was created by Daryl Guppy, a renowned share trader and bestselling author, who came up with the idea of using two distinct groups of moving averages to glean information about market fluctuations.

A group of moving averages is defined as being in an uptrend when the shorter moving averages in the group are above the longer. The primary price trend is determined by the investor group; if the investor group is in an uptrend, the moving averages are coloured green to denote that the primary trend is upward. The secondary trend is determined by the trader group; if the trader group is in an uptrend, the moving average lines are coloured light blue (provided the primary trend is also upward). These two trends are used to determine the direction and strength of the weekly price trend.

The weekly price trend is upward when the following criteria are met:

1. the primary trend is upward (i.e., investor moving averages are green),

2. the trader group is above the investor group of moving averages,

3. the latest weekly candlestick is above the long-term (investor) group of moving averages.

The weekly price trend is strongly upward when, in addition to the above criteria:

4. the investor moving averages are rising at an upward angle and are not close to horizontal, and

5. the price width of the investor group of moving averages is widening or remains wide, signalling trend strength.

Conversely, a group of moving averages is defined as being in a downtrend when the shorter moving averages in the group are below the longer. If the investor group is in a downtrend, the moving averages are coloured red and the primary trend is downward. If the trader group is in a downtrend, the moving average lines are coloured orange (provided the primary trend is also downward).

The weekly price trend is downward when the following criteria are met:

1. the primary trend is downward (i.e., investor moving averages are red),

2. the trader group is below the investor group of moving averages,

3. the latest weekly candlestick is below the long-term (investor) group of moving averages.

The weekly price trend is strongly downward when, in addition to the above criteria:

4. the investor moving averages are falling at a downward angle and are not close to being horizontal, and

5. the price width of the investor group of moving averages is widening or remains wide, signalling trend strength.

The weekly price trend is classified as a sideways (directionless) trend when the weekly price trend is not upward or downward.

Example

Figure 13.2 shows the FTSE 100 during May 2018. The primary trend is upward (as the long-term group has turned green) and the trader group of moving averages is above the investor group. The last weekly candlestick closed above the long-term group of moving averages. The investor group of moving averages are rising on an upward trajectory and have started to widen, suggesting a strong upward trend. That said, prices have reached an area of price resistance, so some caution is needed.

Market direction and stages of the price cycle

The transition in the primary trend for a market index can be used to define stages in the market price cycle.

When the primary trend changes from downward to sideways a *bottoming stage* (stage 1) is formed. When this stage has lasted for several weeks you can start to allow light buying of shares, while waiting for price recovery. The longer the bottoming stage occurs for, the more pronounced the recovery part of the cycle is likely to be. Buying value or income shares is preferred at this stage of the cycle, as they tend to afford more downside protection than growth shares.

Stage 2 of the price cycle is the *recovery stage*, where the primary trend transitions from sideways to upwards. Most of your share buying should occur in this stage.

In the first few weeks of stage 2 the preference is to buy value and income shares. You should transition to buying growth shares, once the trend has been established for several weeks and has cleared any nearby horizontal price resistance. This is usually accompanied by improving earnings growth.

The *topping out stage* (stage 3) occurs when the primary trend transitions from upwards to sideways. The trend may be consolidating before it continues an upward trend (back to stage 2) or the sideways trend may be followed by a downward trend, initiating a *downward stage* (stage 4).

During the *downward stage* (stage 4) you may start to see some sell signals in your portfolio as share prices start to fall and hit their sell stops (see chapter 14 for selling rules). This is useful as it moves some of your portfolio into cash ready to take advantage of new opportunities when the price cycle changes, while helping to limit portfolio losses.

When the overall market is in the *downward stage* (stage 4) no buying of shares is allowed until a bottoming stage has formed, as share prices tend to get dragged down together regardless of the fundamentals. Use this time to research companies that you might want to invest in and prepare for when you can start to buy again.

Example

Figure 13.3 shows over five years of price history for the FTSE 100 and the transitions between the different stages of the price cycle. The FTSE 100 is currently in a stage 2 uptrend, indicating that company share prices in this market are broadly rising and that additional positions can be added. However, caution is needed as the FTSE 100 is approaching a major price resistance level.

Figure 13.3 Trend transitions – FTSE 100

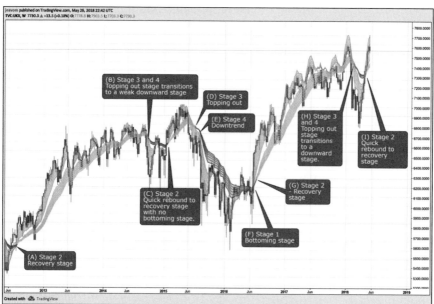

Source: Trading View (tradingview.com)
www.theequityedge.com/wp-content/uploads/2020/02/Figure-13.3.png

Company share price direction

The weekly chart is used to assess the broad price direction for a company. In general, you should prefer investing in companies where the weekly price trend is upward and avoid those trending downward.

Example

Figure 13.4 shows the weekly price chart for XP Power. The investor group is in an uptrend and the trader group of moving averages is above that of the investor group. However, the candlestick is resting on the investor group of moving averages, so the weekly trend is currently defined as sideways. This suggests waiting until prices move higher.

Figure 13.4 Weekly chart – XP Power

Source: Trading View (tradingview.com)
www.theequityedge.com/wp-content/uploads/2020/02/Figure-13.4.png

Daily chart set-up

Daily price charts are used to assess the daily price trend and make buy and sell decisions, having already accounted for the weekly price trend of the company.

Daily candlestick charts

Daily candlestick charts are used to represent the range of prices shares traded at each day. The body of each candlestick shows the area between the open and close of a day, while the area between the high and low of the candlestick shows the overall price range. The shadows of a candlestick show where price traded outside of the open and close price range.

Moving averages

On a daily chart, the short-term group of moving averages consists of three-, five-, eight-, ten-, 12- and 15-day moving averages, while the long-term group consists of 30-, 35-, 40-, 45-, 50- and 60-day moving averages.

Example

Figure 13.5 shows the daily chart for XP Power towards the end of May 2018.

Figure 13.5 Daily chart – XP Power

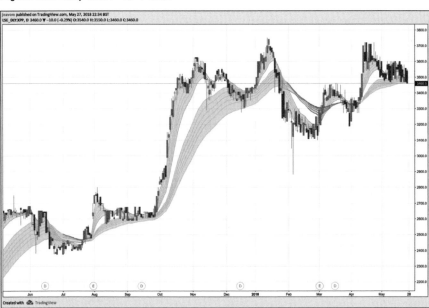

Source: Trading View (tradingview.com)
www.theequityedge.com/wp-content/uploads/2020/02/Figure-13.5.png

Defining the daily trend using daily moving averages

The daily trend is defined in the same way as the weekly trend. The only differences are that the moving averages are based on daily closing prices (instead of weekly closing prices) and different moving average periods are used in the two groups.

When the daily price trend is upward, the purchase of company shares is allowed. When the daily trend is sideways, company shares can be bought when they are close to a key level of support and provided the weekly trend is upward. When both the daily and weekly trend are sideways it is worth waiting until an upward trend establishes itself. If the daily trend is downward, no buying of company shares is allowed.

Example

In figure 13.5 the daily primary trend is upward. The short-term group of moving averages is moving downwards and is meshed with the long-term group of moving averages, indicating the daily trend is currently sideways. The weekly price trend is also sideways, which suggests waiting for an upward price trend to resume.

Identifying support and resistance levels

Prices are dynamic, reflecting the continuing change in the balance between supply and demand. Identifying the price levels at which these balances may change is useful as they help plan the price levels at which to buy or sell shares.

Horizontal support

Horizontal support levels (or floors) represent the price levels where the price tends to find support. This means the price is more likely to move upwards off the level rather than break through it. The more often a level is tested (touched and bounced off by price), the more significant the support level.

If price moves significantly below a support level, it is likely to continue falling until it finds a lower support level and the trend changes. When price breaks significantly below a support level, it becomes a resistance level.

Normally the nearest three horizontal support levels relative to the current price are identified. These are referred to as S1, S2 and S3 (where S1 is above S2 and S2 is above S3) for convenience. Stop losses (discussed in chapter 14) should ideally be placed below S1 or S2, where possible.

Example

Figure 13.6 shows the horizontal support lines for XP Power on the daily chart. The horizontal support levels are S1 = 3102p, S2 = 2762p and S3 = 2560p.

Figure 13.6 Support and resistance levels – XP Power

Source: Trading View (tradingview.com)
www.theequityedge.com/wp-content/uploads/2020/02/Figure-13.6.png

Horizontal resistance

Horizontal resistance levels are the opposite of horizontal support levels. They represent the price levels where the price tends to find resistance. This means that the price is more likely to move downwards off these levels rather than break through it. However, if the price moves significantly above a resistance level, price is likely to continue rising until it finds the next level of resistance and the trend changes. The previous resistance level becomes a support level.

If you are considering buying a company and the price is currently near a horizontal resistance level, you may want to wait until there is either a breakout above resistance or a pullback to support.

Example

Figure 13.6 shows the nearest horizontal resistance for XP Power is R1 = 3741p. This is the highest price level XP Power has achieved and consequently higher resistance levels are not specified.

Trend support and resistance

If the primary trend is upward, the investor group of moving averages, that is, the green ribbon, can be treated as an area of price support. Conversely, if the investor group is in a downtrend, the red ribbon can act as an area of resistance. If the investor group is in a sideways trend, the horizontal support and resistance of the trading range can be used instead.

Example

Figure 13.6 shows the primary trend is currently upward, and that the investor group of moving averages can currently be thought of as resistance. The current trend support level is 3463.6p, which is the lower edge of the ribbon. The closing share price is slightly below this at 3460p. This suggests that the trend may be about to move lower and that a wait and see approach should be adopted.

Buying strategies

Strategy 1 – Buying dips in an uptrend

When a company's share price is trending upwards, a short-term dip in price may provide a useful opportunity to begin buying shares in a company or add to current holdings. This strategy is applicable to income, value and growth companies.

This strategy should only be applied to companies where the weekly and daily trends are upward.

Step 1 – Identifying a short-term dip (set-up)

The first step in this strategy is to identify when a short-term dip has occurred. A short-term dip starts when the daily primary trend remains upward but the daily secondary trend transitions from upwards to sideways. When this happens, the trader group of moving averages changes colour, from blue to grey.

Step 2 – Look for the short-term dip to end (trigger)

Once the dip has started you should wait until the width of the trader group of moving averages has compressed and there is a signal that the downward move in price has ended. This helps to lower the risk of buying into a dip that then turns into a potentially costly downtrend.

The short-term dip is determined to have ended when the secondary trend begins moving upward again. When this happens, the trader group of moving averages turns blue.

Step 3 – Determining a buy price (entry)

Once the secondary trend is upwards the shares can be bought the following day, provided the daily primary trend remains upward.

You should aim to purchase shares at a price that lies within or close to the trader group of moving averages on the day of purchase.

Example

Figure 13.7 shows the daily candlestick chart for XP Power, with the steps applied in an actual share purchase in 2017. The share price was in a strong upward trend when a short-term dip started on 24 February 2017. Several days later the secondary trend turned upward, triggering the trade on 7 March 2017. The shares were purchased the following day at 1928p, a price close to the bottom of the trader group range.

Figure 13.7 Daily chart – XP Power

Source: Trading View (tradingview.com)
www.theequityedge.com/wp-content/uploads/2020/02/Figure-13.7.png

Step 4 – When to sell the shares bought (exit)

The rules for selling an investment holding are discussed in the next chapter. The rules include guidelines on setting the initial protective stop, i.e., the price level at which a decision to sell a company's shares will be made to limit further losses should the current share price fall below it.

Typically, a 20% fall in share price will warrant the selling of shares. The additional rules in chapter 14 should always be applied to companies selected using the income or value screens.

You may want to use tighter protective stops for companies that have been selected using the growth screen, as price falls for growth shares can be more pronounced when the trend changes. In this case, you can set the initial stop just below the investor group of moving averages. Alternatively, the stop loss can be set 8–10% below the breakeven price. You then follow all other rules outlined in chapter 14.

Example

Figure 13.8 shows the horizontal support and resistance levels at the time of the trade. The nearest horizontal support level is S1 = 1874p. On the entry day, the trend support level (determined by the lower edge of the investor group of moving averages) is 1856p.

XP Power is an income company with some growth characteristics. The trend had been in place for some time, so a tight stop was used. The shares were purchased at a breakeven price of 1928p, which means a 10% stop loss would be 1735.2p (= 0.9 × 1928p). However, this was well below the nearest horizontal and trend support levels, so a stop loss of 1854p, the lower bound of the investor moving average ribbon, was chosen instead.

Figure 13.8 Daily chart – XP Power

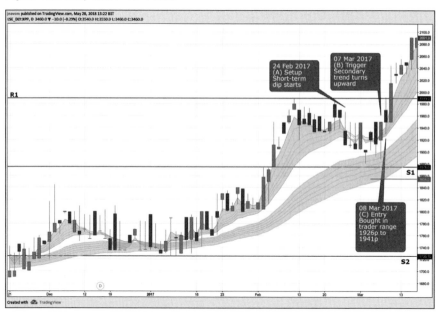

Source: Trading View (tradingview.com)
www.theequityedge.com/wp-content/uploads/2020/02/Figure-13.8.png

Strategy 2 – Buying in a strong uptrend

When a company's share price is trending strongly upwards relative to the overall market, the share price is likely to continue to rally upwards for some time with few pullbacks to take advantage of. Identifying strong upward price trends provides an opportunity to ride the price momentum and generate capital gains. This strategy is often applicable to growth companies.

This strategy requires the daily trend to be strongly upward while the weekly trend is either upward or strongly upward.

Step 1 – Identifying a strong uptrend with relative strength against benchmark (set-up)

This strategy can only be applied to companies where the weekly and daily trend are strongly upward.

Example

Figure 13.9 shows the weekly price chart for XP Power with the weekly analysis applied for an actual share purchase in 2017. The week ending 2 October saw the price rise breakout above 2700p. The weekly price trend is strongly upward, as the investor group of moving averages is widening and rising at an upward angle.

Figure 13.9 Weekly price chart – XP Power

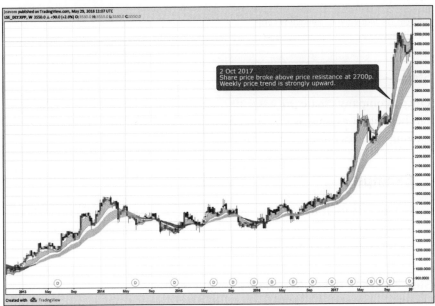

Source: Trading View (tradingview.com)
www.theequityedge.com/wp-content/uploads/2020/02/Figure-13.9.png

Figure 13.10 shows the daily price chart for XP Power with the steps applied in an actual share purchase in 2017. On 2 October, the daily price trend was strongly upward with a widening primary trend rising at an upward angle.

Figure 13.10 Daily price chart – XP Power

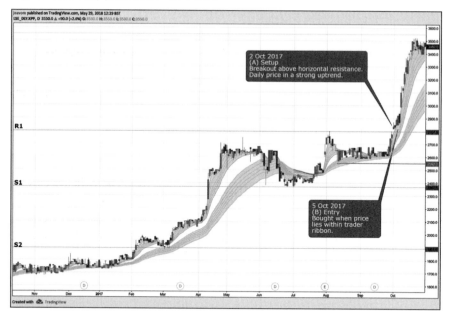

Source: Trading View (tradingview.com)
www.theequityedge.com/wp-content/uploads/2020/02/Figure-13.10.png

Step 2 – Determining a buy price (entry)

Once a company's share price is confirmed to be in a strong uptrend, the shares can be bought as long as the quoted buy price lies within the trader group of moving averages on the day of purchase.

Example

In figure 13.10, it took a few days for the price to trade within the trader group of moving averages. The shares were eventually bought on 5 October 2017 at a breakeven price of 2854p.

Step 3 – When to sell the shares bought (exit)

The rules for exiting are like the previous strategy. However, a tighter protective stop is typically used. The initial stop loss is normally set just below the investor group of moving averages on the day of entry or 8–10% below the breakeven price. You then follow the trailing stop rules proposed in chapter 14 to determine the exact exit.

Example

The nearest horizontal support at the time of purchase was R1 at 2797p, as the price rose above resistance, which then became a support level. The next horizontal support was at S1 at 2367p. The lower bound of the investor group of moving averages was 2640p on the day of purchase.

The breakeven price was 2854p. The 8% stop loss level is therefore 2625.7p (= 0.92 × 2854p), while the 10% stop loss level is 2568.6p (= 0.9 × 2854p). These stop levels are below R1 but above S1. The final stop loss was therefore set at 2552p so that it was below a natural level of support observed on the chart; this moved the stop closer to S1.

Strategy 3 – Buying support during sideways trading

If a company's share price is trending sideways, buying at a price close to a horizontal support level is a good way to minimise early price downside while the sideways move continues. If the market is in a recovery stage, it may also provide an early opportunity to benefit from a share price rise due to a general market recovery.

This strategy is normally applied to income and value companies. For growth companies, the preference is to buy companies with upward price trends that reflect improving earnings over time. For this reason, strategies 1 and 2 are usually preferred for growth companies.

Step 1 – Identifying a sideways price trend

The set-up for this strategy requires that the company's share price is moving sideways in a range. A company's share price is determined to be trending sideways when the daily trend is sideways and the long-term group of moving averages are relatively compressed.

Example

Figure 13.11 shows another trade in XP Power, which qualifies as an income investment. The price started to trend sideways on 6 June 2017 and was eventually confirmed by the primary trend on 3 July 2017.

Step 2 – Determine the trading range

Once a company's share price is determined to be trading sideways, the next step is to determine the trading range. The bottom of the trading range is determined by the nearest confirmed horizontal support level (S1), while the top is determined by the nearest confirmed horizontal resistance level (R1).

Ideally you will want the top of the trading range to be at least 10% higher than the bottom. This ensures that the trading range is wide enough to profit from.

Example

Examining the chart, horizontal support is S1 = 2371p and resistance is R1 = 2752p. The distance between horizontal support and resistance is 381p. The resistance level is 16% higher than the support level, which is wide enough for a trade to be placed.

Step 3 – Wait for the price to close above the investor group of moving averages

Once a sideways price trend has been identified, you need to wait until the price closes above the investor group of moving averages. This signals a bounce from support is confirmed and the shares can be bought the following day.

Figure 13.11 Weekly price chart – XP Power

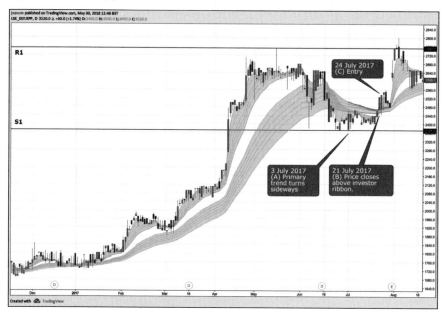

Source: Trading View (tradingview.com)

www.theequityedge.com/wp-content/uploads/2020/02/Figure-13.11.png

Example

The price closes at 2526.1p on 21 July 2017. The distance to support is 155.1p (= 2526.1p – 2371p) and the distance to resistance is 225.9p (= 2752p – 2526.1p), so there is still more upside than downside.

Step 4 – Determining a buy price (entry)

Once the price closes above the investor group of moving averages the shares can be bought the following day, provided the price lies within the bottom third of the trading range.

Example

The shares were purchased the following day at a breakeven price of 2480p. The distance to support is 109p (= 2480p – 2371p) and the distance to resistance is 272p (= 2752p – 2480p). The upside to downside ratio is a healthy 2.5 (= 272 ÷ 109) and the buy price lies within the lower third of the trading range. That is, it lies within 127p (= 381p ÷ 3) of support S1.

Step 5 – When to sell the shares bought (exit)

To sell the shares, you can follow the selling guidelines outlined in the next chapter. However, additional (optional) price-based selling rules can be applied when the share price is at extremes of the trading range.

If the share price falls below 97% of the bottom or rises to the top eighth of the trading range, the shares can be voluntarily sold.

If the share price rises to the top eighth of the trading range and isn't sold, and subsequently falls back to the middle of the trading range, you can again optionally decide to sell the shares; typically this will allow you to take a few percentage points of profit, while allowing you to set-up for another trade at a better price.

Example

The bottom of the trading range is 2371p. Thus, if the share price falls below 2299.9p (= 0.97 × 2371p) the shares can be sold. This helps to keep losses small.

An eighth of the trading range is 47.6p (= 381p ÷ 8). The top eighth of the trading range is therefore 2704.4p (= 2752p – 47.6p) to 2752p. If the price trades above 2704.4p, the shares can be voluntarily sold for a profit.

Summary

Before buying shares in a company you should always use price charts. Looking at price charts allows for price trends to be identified, which incorporate a reflection of fundamental news and market psychology.

When the market is trending downwards share prices will tend to fall together as market sentiment is bearish. During these periods you can partially avoid large drawdowns in portfolio value, which ultimately adds to overall returns. This can lead to significant outperformance relative to the market over the long term.

Similarly, when a company's share price is in a downtrend, the price will often continue to fall. Buying in a downtrend is therefore likely to lead to unnecessary losses. It is far better to wait for the trend to reverse, buying in at a low price with less downside risk, or to look at other companies that are trending upwards and have better price momentum.

This chapter has outlined three strategies to buy shares at an advantageous time. The aim of these strategies is to limit the short-term downside risk and take advantage of positive price momentum, which makes it more likely that an investment will move into profit.

CHAPTER 14

WHEN TO SELL SHARES

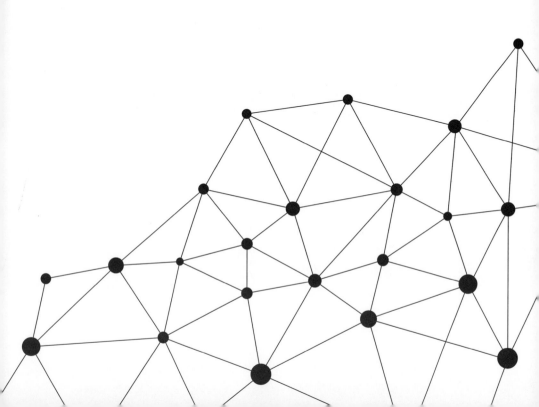

Introduction

T HIS CHAPTER OUTLINES some simple rules for deciding when to sell shares. It is hoped that these rules will provide a systematic process to guide decision making and help avoid common investment mistakes.

The selling rules are applied immediately to company shares that have been bought with a known breakeven buy price. This ensures you know exactly when to sell, while removing the uncertainty and stress involved with making this decision. The only thing you have to commit to is selling company shares when the rules tell you to do so.

Know when to cut your losses

Use a stop loss

When a company's share price starts to fall, it is not uncommon to see people hold on to shares in the hope that the price will eventually recover and breakeven. This allows investments to move from moderate losses to large losses, which can damage portfolio returns.

By failing to realise a loss at the right time, your investment portfolio loses in two ways. First, you fail to sell loss-making investments before losses become large. When a company's share price continues to fall it can create larger and larger losses that are hard to recover from.

Second, there is an opportunity cost of holding on to loss-making shares as the money invested could have been better invested elsewhere. You therefore want to sell shares in any company that starts to make large losses, both to limit further downside risk and preserve portfolio value.

Conversely, selling too early is also a mistake many investors make. When a company's share price falls by a small amount it is tempting to sell the shares immediately; however, this does not allow the company enough time to prove its worth and make a profit. Small movements in price may simply be due to market noise, rather than the idiosyncratic fundamentals of the company.

Selling loss-making shares too quickly on a regular basis can result in too much investment turnover, which increases total transaction cost and hurts portfolio return. You therefore want to ensure that when cutting losses, you are not doing so prematurely.

While price does not dictate the underlying value of a company, if the price has fallen by 20% after purchase there is a strong likelihood that the share price will continue to fall. To limit damage to the portfolio it is advocated to sell holdings where a 20% price drop has occurred. At this point, investment in the company was probably a mistake as large falls in price mean something has gone wrong or has changed and made the investment less appealing or riskier.

Example

Suppose 625 shares of a company are purchased at £4.75 a share. To calculate the breakeven share price, you need to calculate the total cost of the investment, including the stamp duty and transaction costs.

The total value of the shares purchased is £2968.75 (= 625 × £4.75). Stamp duty is charged on share purchases at 0.5% and therefore the stamp duty cost is £14.84 (= 0.5% × £2968.75).

Suppose the transaction cost to buy or sell shares is £12.50, then the round-trip cost of buying and eventually selling later is £25 (= 2 × £12.50).

Thus, the total cost of the investment is £3008.59 (= £2968.75 + £14.84 + £25).

The breakeven share price is the total cost of the investment divided by the number of shares purchased. Thus, the breakeven share price is £4.82 (= £3008.59 ÷ 625), rounded up to the nearest penny.

If the share price falls by 20% from the breakeven price the shares will be sold. That is, if the share price reaches or falls below £3.86 (= (1 − 0.20) × £4.82 = 0.80 × £4.82), the shares will be sold. This price level is commonly referred to as the 'stop loss' level or 'stop' for short.

Choosing a 20% stop loss will typically ensure that you are firmly outside of the market noise when a stop loss is hit and that it is more likely to be investor sentiment over the fundamentals of the company that is driving the fall in share price.

Some investors may question whether a 20% stop loss is too large. After all, a 20% fall in the share price means you need a return of 25% in order to recover the initial amount invested. However, the loss should really be considered in relation to the overall portfolio value.

As you will see in the next chapter, combining stop losses with equity allocation rules ensure that, in the worst-case scenario, no more than 15% of the portfolio value is truly at risk at any point in time. That said, you should start to consider whether to sell the shares once the share price has fallen by 15%.

At a 15% price drop, you should re-assess the investment. If the company shares would no longer be considered for the buy list, you can voluntarily sell; but if the shares are still worth buying, then you should keep hold of them. However, if the price continues to fall and reaches the 20% stop level, the shares should be sold immediately.

Sometimes when you come to sell loss-making shares in a company, you will find that the shares remain on the buy list and the potential returns look enticing. In this case, you should still sell the shares and look to possibly buy them back at a later stage, once downward price momentum appears to have eased. However, one should carefully assess whether the investment case still holds before doing so.

The 20% stop loss is suitable for shares selected for their income or value. However, for growth shares, a tighter stop loss can be used. In this case, one could consider using a simple stop loss that is a few percentage points below the share price low of the previous two or three weeks. Alternatively, you may decide to place the stop a few percentage points below an identified support level. Most stops used for growth shares are in the 10% to 15% range.

Use a time stop loss

Ideally, you should be investing with a minimum investment horizon of three to five years, so that there is no need to react to every market fluctuation. However, if shares are still making a loss (factoring in dividends) after three years of holding them, then there are probably more profitable investment opportunities available.

Growth companies are supposed to be growing earnings rapidly, which should start to drive the price upwards over a three-year period. If a growth company's share price has not risen after three years from the purchase date you should sell the shares.

For shares bought for income, a small loss of capital after three years is bearable, provided the dividend is maintained, as the income stream should eventually be sufficient to offset a small loss. Thus, for income shares, if the shares have made a loss of less than 5% after three years and the dividend has been maintained (or increased) over the period, the shares do not need to be sold. However, if the shares are making more than a 5% loss (once the dividends paid have been factored in) the shares should be sold. Similarly, if an income share is not profitable after three years and the dividend has been cut, the shares should be sold. For loss-making shares that are not sold, you should check the size of the loss and dividend every quarter thereafter.

Companies bought as a value play may need more than three years for their true value to be recognised. Provided the shares remain on the buy list, the time stop can be extended up to five years. However, should the shares no longer be on the buy list at any time after three years, the loss-making shares should be sold immediately. If value shares are still making a loss five years after purchase, they should be sold in order to take advantage of new opportunities.

Example

Suppose a company is an income share purchased at 150p with a dividend yield of 5%. This means each share is expected to provide at least 7.5p in dividends each year.

Three years later, the share price is 120p and 22.5p (= 3 × 7.5p) has been paid out in dividends. Thus, the price including the dividends paid out is 142.5p, which means the shares have made a total loss of 5% (= (142.5 − 150) ÷ 150).

However, a quick check of the underlying fundamentals and broker forecasts suggests that the dividend is unlikely to be cut. The shares are not sold at the end of the three-year period and the sell decision will be re-assessed in three months' time.

Now suppose the dividend was instead cut in the second year to 4p, reducing the total amount of dividends paid out over the three years to 15.5p (= 7.5p + 4p + 4p). The price including the dividend payout is now 135.5p. This would mean the shares have made a loss of 9.7% (= (135.5 − 150) ÷ 150) and should therefore be sold.

Sell if the investment thesis no longer holds

If there are signs of fraud or accounting irregularities it is difficult to make an investment case for holding the shares as the underlying numbers may not be correct. Furthermore, there is an increased likelihood of more negative price shocks ahead. You should therefore sell immediately if there are any signs of fraud or accounting irregularities.

Whether you should sell shares when a profit warning is issued is harder to gauge. For small companies, a profit warning indicates you should sell immediately as there is usually a higher probability of bankruptcy than when larger firms get into difficulties. For large companies (i.e., greater than £1bn) a profit warning is likely to have been priced in very quickly. In this case, assess whether the investment case still holds. If you would still buy the shares today, even if you didn't already have a holding, then it is worth holding on to the shares, since large companies are much more likely to survive and recover over time anyway. However, no further additions to the holding should be made until a full recovery in profits has been made.

Don't fall in love with investments

Too often, when you see a company you have invested in do well, it's easy to fall in love with it and forget that we bought the shares as an investment. At the end of the day, investments need to make money. The quantitative and qualitative analysis should be reviewed at least once a year. If the fundamental investment case for owning shares in a company is no longer viable, you should consider selling the shares.

Know when to take your profits

When company shares become profitable, a common mistake made by investors is to sell and take profits too early. Snatching at profits limits the potential upside and should be avoided.

Conversely, another investment mistake is holding on to shares for too long and letting a large gain turn into a loss. Allowing a profitable investment to fall back into a loss is just not smart, no matter what the reason. You work hard enough to gain an edge in the stock market without allowing the winners to turn into losers. You should aim to run your winners until the share price starts to move against you.

To avoid these mistakes, when a company's share price rises sufficiently you should start to use a trailing stop loss. That is, you should gradually raise your stop loss as the share price rises to reduce risk and eventually remove it entirely.

When the current share price has risen above the breakeven purchase price by 11%, the stop loss should be moved to 2% above the breakeven share price, locking in a little over 18% of the profits made so far. This ensures that you don't let a profit turn into a loss.

Similarly, when the share price has risen above the breakeven price by 15%, the stop loss should be moved to 5% above the breakeven share price. This locks in a third of the profit made so far. The use of these stops ensures that when the price falls by more than 8% you will sell and make a small profit. You can then look to repurchase the shares at a cheaper price later or use the opportunity to rebalance and invest in a company with better prospects.

These stops are appropriate for most large and medium companies, which tend to be less volatile than small companies. The disparity between underlying value and market price tends to be no more than plus or minus 10%.

For companies in certain sectors, such as technology or biotechnology, or for small companies, the proposed stops will not be appropriate as prices tend to be more volatile. You should instead look at the price chart and ensure that your intended stop loss has at least one significant area of horizontal price support between your stop and the current price level. Adjust your percentage stop loss appropriately.

Example

Suppose that shares of a company are bought at a breakeven share price of 200p. At the time of purchase the stop loss is placed 20% below the breakeven share price at 160p (= 0.80 × 200p). The amount risked per share is therefore 40p (= 200p − 160p).

Over the next six months the share price rises 5% to 210p. No action is taken, as you are not going to make the mistake of snatching at small profits. By the end of a 12-month period the share price has risen 11% above the breakeven price, to 222p (= 1.11 × 200p). At this point, the stop loss is moved to 2% above the breakeven price, to 204p (= 1.02 × 200p). This locks in a small profit of around 4p per share, if the price falls back to the stop level.

The share price eventually rises to 230p, which is 15% above the breakeven share price. The stop loss is moved to 5% above the breakeven price to 210p (= 1.05 × 200p). If the share price falls and reaches the stop of 210p, the shares will be sold and a profit of around 10p per share will be made.

Once a company's share price has risen above the breakeven price by 25% or more, the investment is considered to have made a large gain. A trailing stop of 15% is then applied. A trailing stop sets the stop-price level at a fixed percentage below the highest closing price after the purchase date. Trailing stops are only ever moved upwards as new highs are achieved and are **never** moved downwards. Once the price falls below the trailing stop the shares should be sold.

Example

Continuing from the previous example, suppose that the current share price rises to 250p, which is 25% above the breakeven share price of 200p. At this point, the paper profit is 50p (= 250p – 200p) per share. The stop price level is then set 15% below the price high, at 212.5p (= 0.85 × 250p). This locks in a profit of 12.5p per share, which is 25% of the profit made so far.

The share price of the company subsequently rises to 260p, making a new high. The trailing stop is therefore moved up to 221p (= 0.85 × 260p), 15% below the highest closing price since the shares were purchased. If the price subsequently falls to 250p, the stop price level would remain at 221p as the stop level should not be lowered.

Additional rules for selling shares

Sell company shares when they become expensive

When a company share price looks expensive relative to its fundamental value, the potential upside for further price gains is limited. Furthermore, any negative news or underperformance by the company is likely to elicit large falls in the share price. So when shares are identified as being very expensive, it is time to sell them and move the money into new investments which offer greater potential for large returns.

Sell income shares when the current dividend yield falls below 2%

For income shares, you can use the dividend yield as the main measure of value. When the share price rises to the point that the prospective dividend yield is below 2% (i.e., the central banks' long-term inflation level), the shares are considered expensive and you should consider selling. The money from the sale can then be reinvested in shares with a higher dividend yield. Reinvesting the profit also means that there is an additional boost to the amount of income received.

Example

Suppose that 1,500 shares in a company are bought at a breakeven price of 200p per share. At purchase, the shares are expected to pay a dividend of 8p per share over the next 12 months. This is a dividend yield of 4%, so the investment is expected to provide £120 (= 0.04 × 1500 × £2) of income.

Six months later the current share price has risen to 400p. The expected dividend for the following 12 months is now 12p, offering a prospective trailing 12-month dividend yield of 3%. The shares are not sold at this point, as the dividend yield is still above 2% and there is still the possibility of further capital gains.

Six months after that, the share price reaches 600p and the expected dividend for the following 12 months remains at 12p. At this point, the prospective dividend yield has fallen to 2% (= 12p ÷ 600p) so the shares are sold and £9,000 cash is received. The investment has made a capital gain of 200% and over the 12 months paid out a dividend of £120.

If the £9,120 is reinvested at a prospective 4% dividend yield, the investment would be expected to generate £364.80, which is £224.80 more than the previous year. Selling income shares that have become expensive allows you to lock in capital gains and reinvest in higher yielding shares, raising the amount of income that is likely to be received each year.

Note that the dividend yield (defined as dividend per share divided by share price) can fall below 2% if the price goes up substantially or if the dividend yield declines. This rule should only be applied when the yield has fallen due to a rise in price. When applying this rule, if the share price has strong upward momentum you may instead decide to tighten the trailing percentage stop level and sell when the stop is hit. This allows you to take advantage of the upward momentum and exit when this comes to an end.

Sell income shares when the current PE ratio is over 20

A second measure of value is the price to earnings (PE) ratio. When the share price rises to the point that the PE ratio is above 20, the shares are considered expensive and you can choose to sell provided the dividend yield is below 4%. Again, this allows you to take advantage of reinvesting the profits to obtain a higher income stream. If the dividend yield is still above 4% and looks well covered, the company shares are still fulfilling their role as an income share and do not need to be sold.

Example

Suppose a company is purchased at a breakeven price of 100p. For the next 12 months the earnings per share (EPS) is expected to be 10p and the dividend per share (DPS) is 5p. This means that the shares are trading on a forward PE ratio of 10 (= 100p ÷ 10p) and a dividend yield of 5% (= 5p ÷ 100p).

If the share price subsequently rises to 200p and the expected EPS and DPS remain constant, the forward PE ratio will rise to 20 (= 200p ÷ 10p) and the current dividend yield will fall to 2.5% (= 5p ÷ 200p). The shares are therefore viewed as expensive and can be sold.

Sell growth shares when the PEG ratio is over 3

For growth shares, we try to buy company shares with real earnings growth at a reasonable price. If earnings growth falters or the growth potential is fully valued in the share price, the shares are considered to be expensive. The forward PEG ratio (which is the forward PE ratio divided by the expected earnings growth over the next 12 months) is used as a measure of growth at a reasonable price. When the share price rises to the point that the forward PEG ratio is above 3, the shares are considered expensive and can be sold.

Sell value shares when three out of five value measures signal the shares are expensive

Five value measures are used to judge whether value shares have become expensive. The value measures used are: the price to earnings (PE) ratio, the price to tangible book value (PTBV) ratio, price to sales ratio (PSR), price to cash flow (PCF) ratio and enterprise value to EBITDA (EV/EBITDA) ratio.

These measures indicate that company shares have become expensive when: the PE ratio is greater than 20, the PTBV ratio is greater than 5, the PSR is greater than 5, the PCF ratio is greater than 20 or the EV/EBITDA ratio is greater than 12.

When at least three of the five measures indicate that the shares are poor value, the company shares are considered expensive and can be sold. These measures are easy to check on a regular basis as Morningstar publishes the figures daily in their company profiles.

A cut in the dividend may signal a time to sell

Sell income shares when the dividend is cut by 50% or more

When the dividend is cut by more than half it is a strong signal that the company is suffering and may no longer be a reliable dividend payer. Further falls in the share price are likely to occur, so it is worthwhile selling the shares and reinvesting the money in a more secure dividend-paying company.

Sell growth shares if the dividend is cut

For growth shares, the dividend is usually a small proportion of earnings. Nevertheless, maintaining a dividend is a signal of good cash management. If the dividend is cut for a growth share, it may be a signal that there are future problems for the company. In this case, sell the shares if the growth story has changed (e.g., the chairman delivers a downbeat statement for the company) or the outlook based on the numbers looks unfavourable.

Knowing when to buy back in

When an investment in company shares has hit its stop (i.e., the share price has fallen to or below the stop level) the shares are sold and either a profit or loss is made. Reinvestment in the company can eventually be made provided the company is on the buy list, the downward price momentum has stabilised, and the share price has started to rise again.

The share price is judged to have stabilised once the company share price has risen above the high of the previous three weeks and the daily price trend is upward.

Summary

This chapter has outlined a simple set of rules for systematically selling shares. The hope is that by applying these rules you can avoid the behavioural investment mistakes and large losses that accompany them.

In summary, when an investment in company shares is making a loss the shares should be sold when:

1. the share price falls below its trailing stop level (usually set at 20% to start with);

2. the shares are still making a loss (factoring in dividend payments) after three years of holding them (for value companies, this can be extended to five years if the shares remain on the buy list);

3. there is a profit warning or signs of fraud or accounting irregularities.

When an investment in company shares becomes sufficiently profitable, some of the profit should be locked in using trailing stops. When an 11% gain is made, the stop level should be moved 2% above the breakeven price; when a 15% gain is made, the stop should be moved to 5% above the breakeven price. Once a 25% gain has been made, a 15% trailing stop should be used.

If company shares become overvalued the shares can be sold and the money reinvested in cheaper, more profitable shares. For income shares, this occurs when the forward dividend yield falls below 2% or the PE ratio rises above 20. For growth shares, this occurs when the PEG ratio is more than 3. For value shares, a number of value metrics need to be signalling the shares are expensive before being sold. When there is positive price momentum, an alternative to selling immediately is to tighten the trailing stop levels and sell when they are hit.

A cut in the dividend may also signal that it is time to sell. If an income company cuts its dividend by more than half (or a growth company cuts its dividend) it is a sign to look for higher yielding companies (or the earning growth story may be in trouble). It's therefore time to sell.

CHAPTER 15

MANAGING INVESTMENT ALLOCATION

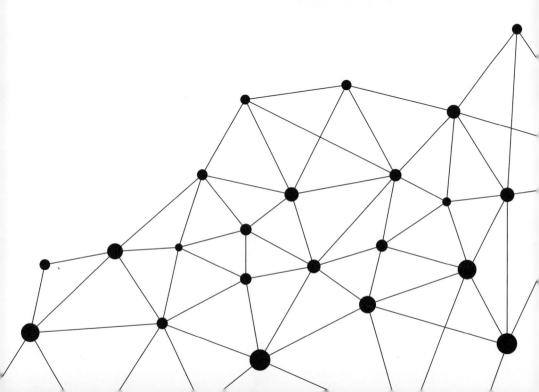

Introduction

M ANAGING INVESTMENT ALLOCATION within the portfolio is one of the most important aspects of investing successfully in the stock market. Despite this, most investment books available overlook this. As a result, few people understand the implications and benefits of managing investment allocation within the portfolio.

Previous chapters have described how to combine fundamental and technical analysis to improve the odds of making consistent positive returns. However, investing is a game of averages and at times there will be periods of loss.

Managing investment allocation helps produce a well-balanced portfolio that is structured to limit potential losses at any point in time. This ensures the portfolio does not become overextended to the point that a large loss (or a general downturn in the market) damages long-term investment returns.

It achieves this by specifying rules on the maximum amount that can be invested in a company, sector or region, relative to the overall size of the portfolio. In addition, allocating money and investments across different accounts allows you to make the most of tax allowances. Reducing the amount paid on taxes will help improve return.

Specific investment risk

Investing too large a proportion of your overall portfolio in a single company is the most frequent reason for portfolio values being severely damaged. To understand why this is the case, consider table 15.1, which shows the percentage gain required to recover from different sized losses.

Table 15.1 Portfolio return required to recover from a loss

Size of loss (%)	Percentage gain required to recover from the loss	Years taken to recover at 7% return per annum	Years taken to recover at 10% return per annum
5%	5.3%	1	1
10%	11.1%	2	1
15%	17.6%	2	2
20%	25.0%	3	2
25%	33.3%	4	3
50%	100.0%	10	7
75%	300.0%	20	15
90%	900.0%	34	24
100%	Never	Never	Never

The first point to note is that the return required to recover from a loss is always bigger than the percentage loss made. For example, a 10% loss would require the portfolio to return 11.1% to fully recover. Thus, an extra 1.1% return is required to regain the original portfolio value prior to the loss.

The second point to note is that the return required to recover from a loss increases exponentially as the relative size of the initial loss increases. This means that the bigger the loss, the longer and harder the remaining assets will have to work for the portfolio to return to its original value.

The third column of the table shows the number of years (rounded up to the nearest year) that it would take to recover from different sized losses based on an annual return of 7% per annum in the future. (Here, we assume the long-term market average return from investing a lump sum in the stock market is 7% per annum.) A loss of more than 20% will take more than three years for the portfolio to recover.

Consider the extreme case of a portfolio being fully invested in a single company. Should the company become worthless overnight you would lose all the money invested and be unable to recover without additional money being added. Of course, complete bankruptcy of a company is an extreme event which is less likely to happen if you follow the advice in previous chapters and select companies that have strong balance sheets.

However, one-off company-specific events can sometimes severely damage a company's value overnight. For example, BP's share value plummeted by almost 50% after its Deepwater Horizon oil rig exploded and sank in May 2010. The disaster resulted in one of the largest accidental marine oil spills in the history of the petroleum industry and left BP with substantial costs to cover the environmental and economic damage that had been caused. If the whole portfolio was invested in BP, it would take around a decade for the portfolio to recover, assuming a 7% return per annum return was subsequently realised (see table 15.1).

Alternatively, if 50% of the portfolio had been invested in BP at the time of the disaster, the initial portfolio loss would have been around 25% of the portfolio value. The portfolio would then have had to return 33.3% to recover from the loss, which would take four years, assuming a 7% return per annum. By investing a lower percentage of the portfolio in any one company, the specific company loss is limited and recovery times are improved.

Consequently, if you fully invest in too few companies, such that you take large positions relative to your portfolio, and they start to lose money, it is entirely possible for the value of the portfolio to be severely damaged by big losses which will take a long time to recover from. You should therefore limit the amount invested in any one company.

For portfolios worth less than £500,000, the largest proportion of the portfolio allowed to be invested in a single company is 5%

For example, if the portfolio value was £100,000, then no more than 5% of the portfolio value can be invested in a single company. Put another way, the portfolio should hold no more than £5,000 in the shares of any one company. This ensures that if a company becomes worthless the loss is limited to 5%. The remaining portfolio should be able to recover from this loss in under a year, all other things being equal.

Note, for small portfolios worth less than £20,000, the investable amount is set at £1,000, as otherwise trading costs become too high relative to the amount invested.

For portfolios worth between £500,000 and £1m, the largest amount of the portfolio allowed to be invested is £25,000. This keeps the proportion allocated between 2.5% and 5%

Keeping the maximum investment in a company limited to £25,000, allows the largest percentage invested in a single company to transition from 5% to 2.5%. This allows the portfolio to become more diversified as it grows in size.

For portfolios worth more than £1m, the largest proportion of the portfolio allowed to be invested in a single company is 2.5%

This limits the number of companies in the portfolio to 40, striking a balance between the benefits of diversification and the benefits to returns from a concentrated portfolio.

When the above rules are combined with the techniques discussed in previous chapters, the chance of a significant loss is reduced. For example, if a 20% stop loss is implemented (as suggested in the previous chapter) there is a good chance that the actual loss will be lower. For example, if 5% of a portfolio is invested in a company and the share price falls below the stop price and is sold, the actual loss may be limited to around 1% of the portfolio value, which can be easily recovered.

Sector risk

Sector risk is the risk that many of the companies in a sector (such as financials, health care, basic materials and so forth) will fall in price at the same time because of an event that affects the entire industry.

In this case, price movements in companies within a sector become more correlated (i.e., they tend to move together more) and losses can be compounded. For example, the collapse in crude oil price from over $115 in June 2014 to under $30 at the beginning of 2016 led to sharp falls in value for companies in, or associated with, the energy sector. You therefore want to be well diversified across sectors over time.

To limit the impact of a negative sector event, no more than 20% of the portfolio value can be invested in any one sector. This ensures that in the worst-case scenario, where all of the companies in a sector suddenly become worthless overnight, the loss in portfolio value will be limited to 20%. Better still, should a negative sector event occur, the use of a 20% stop loss means that there is a good chance that the overall loss would be limited to around 4% of the portfolio. A loss of around 4% should be recoverable within a year, assuming an average future return of 7% per annum.

Of course, the above assumes that only one sector is affected. In some cases, a negative event may affect one or more sectors. If more sectors are affected, the potential losses could be larger but would still be limited to no more than 20% of the total portfolio, due to the use of the 20% stop loss. In this extreme case, it would take around three years for the portfolio to recover, if future returns averaged 7%.

Position risk

Position risk is the percentage of the portfolio value that is potentially at risk of loss from an investment in a single company, should its stop loss be hit. (The possibility of a catastrophic event that collapses the value of a company too quickly for a stop loss to be effective is excluded – this risk is dealt with in the specific investment risk section.) Limiting position risk to a reasonable level helps to reduce losses from any one company.

The initial position risk can be calculated by multiplying the percentage stop loss and the amount invested in the company (to obtain the value of the position that is at risk of loss) and then divide by the current value of the portfolio.

For portfolios worth less than £500,000, the maximum position risk allowed is 2%

For portfolios between £500,000 and £1m the maximum position risk is set at £10,000

The maximum position risk allowed in percentage terms starts at 2% for portfolios valued at £500,000 and steadily declines to 1% as the portfolio size approaches £1m.

For portfolios in excess of £1m, the maximum position risk allowed is set at 1%

Using these maximum position risk rules, you can calculate the maximum amount that can be invested in a single company. The amount is calculated by multiplying the position risk by the portfolio value and dividing by the percentage stop loss. Thus, if the stop loss is set at 20% (as recommended in the previous chapter), the maximum amount that can be invested in a single company is five times the position risk multiplied by the portfolio value.

Example

Suppose the current portfolio value is £100,000 and you are considering buying shares in a company. Following the rules, the maximum position risk is set to 2%. This means that the position value at risk of loss is limited to £2,000 (= 0.02 × £100,000). If a 20% stop loss is used, the maximum amount that can then be invested in the company's shares is £10,000 (= 0.02 × £100,000 ÷ 0.20). Note that this is five times the position value at risk.

Changes in position risk

While a position held in a company is making a loss, the position risk will remain the same so you should limit purchases to the total value allowed. However, once the shares have risen sufficiently in price, a trailing stop can be put in place that is above the breakeven purchase price for the shares. (Deciding how and when to use a trailing stop is covered in the previous chapter; however, a profit will normally be locked in once the share price has risen 11% above the breakeven price.)

Once the stop is above the breakeven price, an expected minimum profit is locked in and the position risk is now zero. This allows an additional position to be added to the company, provided the specific investment and sector risk rules are satisfied. The additional investment amount allowed is based on the value of the portfolio at the time the investment is being considered.

Example

Continuing the previous example, suppose £2,500 was spent on a company and the share price subsequently rises sufficiently for a trailing stop loss above the breakeven price to be put in place. At this point, the current position risk in the company is zero, and a further investment may be added.

Suppose the value of the shares rose by 20% to £3,000, and that a stop loss is now placed above the breakeven price (according to our selling rules, mentioned in the previous chapter). The portfolio value, all other things being equal, has risen to £100,500.

The position risk rule limits you to a 2% position risk, which means that an additional £10,050 (= 0.02 × £100,500 ÷ 0.20) of shares can now be purchased in the company. The specific investment risk rule limits the amount invested in a single company to 5% of the portfolio value, which equates to £5,025 (= 0.05 × £100,500). As £3,000 of the company is already being held in the portfolio, the additional amount that can be purchased is limited to £2,025 (= £5,025 − £3,000).

Portfolio risk

Portfolio risk is the percentage of the overall portfolio value that is potentially at risk from all of the companies invested in, when stop losses are being used. Portfolio risk is therefore the sum of all open position risks. Limiting the amount of portfolio risk helps to protect the portfolio from a catastrophic collapse in market value, where share prices fall together.

Portfolio risk is not allowed to be more than 15% of the total portfolio value. This ensures that a severe market drawdown, which results in share price losses of more than 20%, will typically be limited to around a 15% loss on the portfolio. Referring to table 15.1, a 15% loss on the portfolio can usually be recovered within a few years, assuming an average 7% return per annum.

The number of open positions allowed (assuming that the maximum amount of position risk for each investment is taken) can be calculated by dividing the portfolio risk by the position risk.

Example

If the portfolio value is £100,000, the maximum position risk is 2% and the maximum portfolio risk is 15%. The maximum number of holdings that can still make a loss is therefore 7 (= 15% ÷ 2% = 7.5), which is rounded down to the nearest whole integer.

Using smaller position risk sizes than the maximum allowed permits more open positions to be held. However, in this case, you should cap the number of open positions that can possibly make a loss to 30. This makes it easier to keep track of companies invested in, while managing sell and buy decisions.

Applying the portfolio risk rule means that in down markets the portfolio tends to have a greater proportion in cash; this is because any position entered into at this time will generally remain loss making, so it is better to retain cash rather than buy. In up markets, the portfolio will gradually move towards being fully invested, as portfolio risk will steadily fall as share prices rise, allowing more positions to be added as profits get locked in.

Example

Suppose the initial portfolio value is £100,000, which is held in cash. As in the previous example, portfolio risk will allow up to seven holdings in different companies to be bought.

The specific investment risk rule allows no more than 5% to be invested in any one company, which equates to £5,000.

The position risk allowed is 2% (or £2,000) and combined with a 20% stop loss this implies that the maximum amount that can be invested in a company is £10,000. This is double the specific investment risk allowed.

You therefore take half the maximum position risk allowed for each company invested in. That is, 1% position risk on each trade. Thus, you can invest in up to 15 companies (= 15% ÷ 1%), investing £5,000 in each company. This means that 75% of the portfolio is initially invested in shares and 25% (£25,000) is held in cash.

Suppose that six months later, two of the companies have increased in value by 20% and stop losses have been put in place 5% above their respective breakeven prices; the 13 remaining companies have risen by 5% and their stop loss levels have not been adjusted. This means that the current portfolio value has risen to £105,250 and 76.25% (= (£105,250 – £25,000) ÷ £105,250) of the portfolio is now invested in shares.

Thirteen of the companies still have the same position risk, as their share prices have not risen sufficiently to lock in a profit. Two of the companies have locked in profits, meaning their position risk has gone to zero (i.e., the position risk is closed). Thus, the portfolio risk has fallen from 15% to 13% (= 15% – (2 × 1%)).

The current portfolio value is now £105,250 and the portfolio is carrying a 13% position risk on 15 investments. (The position risk in percentage terms is slightly lower as the portfolio has increased in value; however, it is a convenient approximation to just carry the percentage risk based on initial calculations.)

The specific investment risk rule allows no more than 5% to be invested in any one company, which equates to £5,262.50 (= 0.05 × £105,250). The position risk allowed is 2% (or £2,105) and combined with a 20%

stop loss this implies that the maximum amount that can be invested is £10,525.

This is double the specific equity risk allowed and again half the maximum position risk (1%) is risked on each trade. This means that two new positions can be added, with the maximum value allowed in each holding now being £5,262.50. This raises the percentage of the portfolio invested in shares from 76.25% to 86.25%.

Regional risk

Regional risk is the risk that companies located in a geographical region will fall in price at the same time because of a negative regional event or shock. In this case, price movements in companies within the region become more correlated (that is, they tend to move together more) and losses can be compounded. Ideally the portfolio should be well distributed across different geographic regions to reduce this risk and improve returns on the portfolio.

Diversifying across regions can be problematic when selecting individual shares for the portfolio. This is because you need to have access to share screeners that cover shares listed in multiple regions, which usually incurs additional cost. This is less of an issue for high-value portfolios as the relative costs will be small and the techniques outlined in previous chapters will be easily applied to different regions. However, for low-value portfolios, say under half a million pounds, these extra costs can be prohibitively expensive.

Fortunately, there is a relatively straightforward way to check the degree of geographical diversification a portfolio has. The Morningstar website provides the proportion of revenue generated from each region for every listed company, which is accessible from the company stock profiles. This can be used to calculate the amount of portfolio revenue being generated from each region and the regional exposure of the portfolio. You can then try to diversify the portfolio exposure by selecting companies with exposure to desired regions.

Example

Table 15.2 shows the regional exposure of an example portfolio. The number of shares owned and the sales per share are shown for each company in the portfolio. This allows the amount of company revenue attributable to the shares owned to be calculated. This is done by multiplying the number of shares owned by the current sales per share figure (see column 4).

The regional breakdown of sales is available from the Morningstar company profile page; these are allocated to the relevant categories listed in the table. If Morningstar does not have a regional breakdown, sales are allocated to the UK. (In the example, Aviva and Hansard Global do not have a regional breakdown and sales are allocated to the UK, as this is where the shares are listed.)

Sales by region is calculated by multiplying the proportion of sales generated in a region by the amount of sales owned for each company and summing them up. The second from bottom row shows the amount of sales in each region.

The proportion of sales attributable to each region is calculated in the bottom row of the table. It shows that 75% of portfolio-owned sales are generated within the UK. This is the largest weighting and is to be expected as the initial focus of the portfolio is on UK-listed companies. However, 25% of the portfolio is generated from overseas.

Table 15.2 Calculating regional exposure

Company	No. of Shares	Sales per Share (p)	Sales Owned (£)	UK	US	EU	CAN	AUS	JAP	Other Americas	Other Asia	Africa	Rest of World
Aviva	739	1008	7449.12	100.0%	0.0%	0.0%	0.0%	0.0%	0.0%	0.0%	0.0%	0.0%	0.0%
BP	625	1782	11137.50	0.0%	34.9%	0.0%	0.0%	0.0%	0.0%	0.0%	0.0%	0.0%	65.1%
Braemar Shipping	718	622.3	4468.11	67.6%	0.0%	0.0%	0.0%	4.6%	0.0%	0.0%	18.4%	0.0%	9.4%
Chesnara	1199	622	7457.78	100.0%	0.0%	0.0%	0.0%	0.0%	0.0%	0.0%	0.0%	0.0%	0.0%
Cineworld	1550	281	4355.50	100.0%	0.0%	0.0%	0.0%	0.0%	0.0%	0.0%	0.0%	0.0%	0.0%
Daisy Crest Group	1686	1012	17062.32	96.7%	0.0%	0.0%	0.0%	0.0%	0.0%	0.0%	0.0%	0.0%	3.3%
Glaxo Smith Kline	252	544.9	1373.15	5.8%	32.0%	0.0%	0.0%	0.0%	0.0%	0.0%	0.0%	0.0%	62.3%
Hansard Global	1824	39.5	720.48	0.0%	0.0%	100.0%	0.0%	0.0%	0.0%	0.0%	0.0%	0.0%	0.0%
IG Group	466	111.3	518.66	50.8%	0.0%	21.9%	0.0%	15.4%	4.4%	0.0%	0.0%	0.0%	7.5%
Sainsbury	1000	1196.3	11963.00	100.0%	0.0%	0.0%	0.0%	0.0%	0.0%	0.0%	0.0%	0.0%	0.0%
Tesco	930	840.9	7820.37	67.5%	0.0%	14.5%	0.0%	0.0%	0.0%	0.0%	17.9%	0.0%	0.0%
Vodaphone	1430	89.9	1285.57	11.6%	11.8%	57.8%	0.0%	0.0%	0.0%	0.0%	9.8%	8.9%	0.0%
Sales By Region (£)			56521	4473	2713	0	284	23	0	2352	115	9130
Regional Exposure			74.8%	5.9%	3.6%	0.0%	0.4%	0.0%	0.0%	3.1%	0.2%	12.1%

Rebalancing the portfolio

Over time, the make up of companies in the portfolio will change as share prices rise and fall. Over time, some stocks will increase substantially in value, potentially dominating the portfolio, while others will fall in value. Regularly rebalancing the portfolio helps to ensure that the portfolio remains well balanced across a range of companies.

To achieve a balanced portfolio, the portfolio management rules are applied and checked before buying an additional holding of shares in a company. The rules for selling shares (explained in the previous chapter) are followed and when sales are made, this is taken as an opportunity to rebalance the portfolio as needed. This simple approach ensures trading costs are kept low.

Tax efficiency – Allocating money and shares between different accounts

Reducing the amount of tax paid on investments is key to maximising long-term investment returns. It is therefore essential to make the most of personal tax allowances. In the UK, the key tax allowances are for individual savings accounts (ISA), capital gains, dividends and self-invested personal pensions (SIPP). Efficiently allocating money and shares between trading, ISA and SIPP accounts help to ensure these allowances are taken full advantage of.

Individual savings accounts (ISA)

Investing within an ISA protects your returns from tax, particularly if you are a higher rate taxpayer. Although the exact rules around the benefits have changed over the years, all capital gains made within an ISA account are free from tax and do not deplete your capital gains allowance. This can be particularly useful when you have built up a number of years' worth of ISA investments.

The only downside is that capital losses made within an ISA cannot be used to offset capital gains made outside of the ISA wrapper. In addition, you don't have to pay income tax on any dividends earned from investments held within the share ISA. (Similarly, with cash ISAs you do not have to pay tax on the interest paid.)

For the tax year 2019/20 the ISA allowance for each eligible adult is £20,000. (That is, no more than £20,000 can be paid into the account each year.) This allowance can be used in a stocks and shares ISA, a cash ISA, or both. This allowance must be used within the tax year; any allowance not used by the end of the tax year is lost. The ISA allowance should be the first allowance to be used and you should try to make full use of the allowance every year.

In the UK, income tax rates are higher than capital gains tax (CGT) rates. It is therefore advised that money placed within the ISA is used to purchase a broad range of income and value shares. Doing this ensures that the ISA account will gradually produce a steady stream of income that is both tax-free and growing. As income grows, the portfolio should experience gradual capital gains as well.

Capital gains allowance

Capital gains is a tax levied on the profits from the sale of assets (including shares in an ordinary trading account) that exceed an annual allowance. The capital gains allowance for the 2019/20 tax year is £12,000.

Capital gains in excess of this level are taxed at the standard rate of 10% in the basic income tax band and at the higher rate of 20% for higher and top-rate taxpayers. For the tax year 2019/20, an individual with income up to £50,000 will fall within the basic-rate taxpayer band, while people with taxable income and gains over this will fall within the higher rate taxpayer band.

Example

If an individual sells some shares from their trading account for £20,000, having bought them ten years ago for £4,000, a capital gain of £16,000 is made. After deducting their annual CGT allowance of £12,000, they will be left with a taxable gain of £4,000.

If this falls into the basic-rate tax band the individual must pay 10% tax, i.e., £400 (= 0.10 × £4,000). If the individual is in the higher rate tax band they will instead pay 20%, equal to £800 (= 0.20 × £4,000). If the taxable gain overlaps income tax bands, then the gain within the basic income tax band will be taxed at 10% and the remainder taxed at 20%.

Once the ISA allowance has been used for the tax year, the aim is to then make use of the annual capital gains allowance as much as is practical. To achieve this, additional earned income should be invested in growth and value shares in an ordinary trading account. Shares from the income buy-list are not used as the aim is to make profits through capital gains, rather than income, which is taxable for higher rate taxpayers.

As the value of shares within the trading account increases, it makes sense to strip out gains from within your annual capital gains allowance as the end of the tax year approaches, rather than letting large gains accumulate over a number of years and eventually result in a large tax bill when the shares are eventually sold. (Note that if you sell a particular share, you must wait 30 days before buying it back if you wish to 'trigger' the gain.)

These gains should be transferred to your ISA account each tax year using your ISA allowance. Eventually the growth portfolio will throw off enough cash to fill the ISA each year, creating a virtuous cycle of gains.

Example

Suppose a basic-rate taxpayer owns a range of shares worth £9,000 in their trading account. After five years the shares have doubled in value to £18,000, and after ten years they are worth £26,000.

If the shares are sold in year ten, a £17,000 profit will have been made. Assuming the capital gains allowance is £12,000 (the current figure), the profit is £5,000 above the annual capital gains allowance and a tax bill of £500 (= 10% × £5,000) will need to be paid. Thus, the net profit over the ten years is £16,500.

Alternatively, capital gains can be taken more frequently. If the shares are sold after five years, a profit of £9,000 is made, which is within the annual capital gains allowance and so there is no capital gains tax to pay (assuming there are no other taxable investment gains that tax year). The £18,000 can then be reinvested in other shares and at year ten the portfolio is again worth £26,000. The portfolio is sold and an £8,000 gain is realised, which again is within the annual capital gains allowance. Thus, the net profit over the ten years is £17,000.

From this example, it should be clear that regularly taking gains can save a fortune in capital gains tax over the course of a lifetime. Ideally, capital gains should be taken every few years (and at least once over a five-year period).

Dividend allowance

For the tax year 2019/20, investors have a dividend allowance of £2,000 per person. Dividends in excess of this amount are taxed at 7.5% for basic taxpayers, 32.5% for higher rate taxpayers and 38.1% for top-rate taxpayers (45% income tax band). In addition, the personal savings allowance allows dividends to be protected from tax up to £1,000 per person each tax year. (Higher rate payers get a £500 allowance, and additional rate payers don't get an allowance.)

After using the ISA allowance, the dividend allowance is useful as you can earn some tax-free income in a normal trading account. This allows you to invest in value companies, which payout a dividend, while waiting for capital appreciation as the underlying company value is recognised.

Hold assets jointly

It is worth noting that if you are married or in a civil partnership and living together, you both have individual ISA, capital gains and dividend allowances to make use of. While money in ISAs cannot be transferred between individuals' accounts, assets can be shared across trading accounts for yourself and your partner. This means the capital gains (and losses) can be spread across accounts so that you can make full use of capital gains allowances for both of you.

In addition, if you are earning dividend income, make sure your dividend paying shares are shared with your partner. This is so that you make full use of both allowances and ensure that the partner paying the lowest rate of income tax receives the most dividends.

Inheritance tax

While nobody likes to think about their own death, it is worth considering what would happen to your estate should you die. It is good etiquette to have a will outlining who you would like to inherit your wealth as well as a letter (stored securely) detailing all the accounts and assets held. This is so the full estate is readily identifiable and can be distributed to your loved ones through the administrative process after your death.

There are steps you can take to limit the amount of inheritance tax (IHT) paid. There is currently no inheritance tax to pay where an estate (for example, a house and a portfolio of shares) is inherited by a spouse or a civil partner. Where someone else is inheriting, such as children or a sibling, the inheritance tax is payable at 40% on everything above £325,000, or £650,000 where a married couple (or civil partners) have first left everything to their partner and have not used up the £325,000 that everyone is entitled to pass on tax-free.

In addition, there is a main residence inheritance allowance, which provides additional tax relief for direct descendants (children, stepchildren and grandchildren) inheriting a main residence.

For the 2019/20 tax year, the allowance is £150,000, and is set to rise to £175,000 in 2020/21. This means that a married couple with children will be able to shelter an estate worth up to £1m from inheritance tax, provided a residential property is part of that estate.

It is worth noting that unmarried couples are at a significant tax disadvantage. Neither the standard IHT or the residential IHT can be transferred between unmarried couples. Unmarried couples should therefore aim to each own half of their joint assets so that they can be passed down directly on death.

SIPP

Once the ordinary trading account has started to regularly make capital gains in excess of the capital gains allowance and the ISA allowance is being fully utilised every year, it is worth investing in a self-invested personal pension (SIPP). A SIPP is a tax-efficient pension account where you can hold investments in shares, funds and cash (thus sheltering them from tax), while having the added advantage of tax relief on your contributions.

Assuming that you will mainly want to invest in shares, you should find an execution-only stockbroker that offers a low-cost SIPP account. SIPP costs may include a set-up fee to establish the account, ongoing annual management fees and transaction costs.

It should be possible to find competitive SIPP accounts without a set-up fee that charge no more than 0.5% per annum management fees, subject to a maximum amount payable of a few hundred pounds. Transaction costs for sale and purchase of shares should be in line with those paid in an ordinary trading account.

Money invested in a SIPP can be used to buy and sell shares in the same way as other trading accounts. Like ISAs, no tax is charged on dividends or capital gains made within the account. The key difference though is that money in the SIPP cannot be withdrawn from the pension until you are 55. Even when you reach 55, you can only take out 25% of the pension fund value as a tax-free lump sum, while the remainder is taken as a monthly, taxable income. Furthermore, there are restrictions on how the income can be drawn.

When funds are added to the SIPP, you will receive tax relief from the government and your stockbroker (courtesy of the Inland Revenue) will automatically add tax back at the basic rate. For a basic-rate taxpayer (taxed at 20%), a sum equal to 25% of the amount put into the SIPP will be added. Thus, if you want to add £10,000 to a SIPP you only have to pay in £8,000 and the government will pay in £2,000.

Higher and top-rate taxpayers can claim for higher tax relief each year using the self-assessment tax return system. High-rate taxpayers are entitled to a further 20% rebate, while top-rate taxpayers are entitled to a 25% rebate. This means that for every £100 invested by a high-rate taxpayer, the actual cost to them is only £60; the other £40 being paid by the taxman. Similarly, for top-rate taxpayers, the actual cost is only £55, with £45 contributed by the taxman. The extra relief works by expanding your basic-rate tax band by the amount of the gross pension contribution paid, rather than a physical payment of the extra tax due.

The maximum amount that can be contributed by anyone (yourself or your employer, for instance) into all your pensions in a tax year is dictated by the annual pension allowance. For 2019/20, if you are earning less than £40,000 before tax you are entitled to invest the gross value of your salary in your pension each year. For example, if you earn £35,000, you should be able to contribute £35,000 gross to your pension. The payment you make will be £28,000, to which the taxman will automatically add basic-rate (20%) tax relief of £7,000.

If you earn more than £40,000, you are entitled to contribute up to £40,000 gross to your pension each year. If your earnings are above £150,000, the pension allowance is tapered away by £1 for every £2 of earnings in excess of £150,000. For example, if your earnings were £160,000, your annual pension allowance would be £35,000.

You can use up allowances for the previous three tax years if you have not already done so. Under the carry forward rules, you could add your unused £40,000 allowance for the past three years. If you are a top-rate taxpayer, you could receive relief of up to £54,000 (= 0.45 × £120,000).

Contributions above the annual allowance are taxed as income, unless you carry forward unused allowance from the last three tax years. This annual allowance does not apply to any pension transfers. There is a cap on the size of your pension pot and penalties are employed if you exceed the limit. From April 2019, the lifetime allowance is £1,055,000. While this may seem to be a large amount, many will reach this limit in their lifetime.

If you are investing for retirement, SIPPS are more tax efficient than ISAs. For higher rate taxpayers, no tax is paid on earned money invested in a SIPP due to the tax relief. When money is drawn as an income in retirement from the SIPP, most higher rate taxpayers will revert to becoming low-rate taxpayers and the income will only be taxed at the basic rate, which is currently 20%.

In contrast, earned income is effectively taxed at 40% or 50% on money invested in the ISA (as there is no tax relief on money going into ISAs) and money withdrawn from the ISA is tax-free. The case for basic-rate taxpayers is less clear cut, as the effective tax-rate will remain 20%. However, it is still more tax efficient as the lump sum paid out is tax-free.

Despite SIPPs being more tax efficient, ISAs have four advantages that make them preferable when investing for general purposes:

1. ISAs have lower running costs compared with SIPPs.

2. ISAs allow you to access your money at all times, with no restrictions on what you can do with the money; this means a tax-free income can be drawn at any time.

3. The income generated by an ISA does not need to be entered on a tax return, and therefore does not count towards income calculations for tax purposes.

4. ISAs are simpler and currently less affected by government meddling. For example, the government is currently reducing the amount that can be saved in a pension each year and has lowered the maximum threshold before tax starts to be paid. There are also ongoing discussions about further reducing tax relief for higher rate taxpayers and lowering the proportion of the pension fund value that can be taken as a lump sum.

Such advantages make a compelling case to initially invest in ISAs and only begin to pay into SIPPs in later life, when you can afford to lock away money until you're 55. Due to additional costs, it is only worth investing in a SIPP once you have a lump sum of £25,000 or more available to pay in.

Within a SIPP it is acceptable to invest in income, value and growth shares. For those under the age of 55, a simple strategy is to invest your age divided by 55 of the SIPP portfolio value in income shares and the remainder in value and growth shares. For example, for an investor aged 39, 71% (= 39 ÷ 55) of the portfolio should be invested in income shares and 29% (= 100% − 71%) should be invested in value and growth shares. For those over 55, the portfolio should be completely invested in income shares.

Take financial advice when considering pension options

It is recommended that you consult a financial advisor when thinking about investing in a SIPP. Taking control of your pension ensures there is no 'top slicing' of your investment pot by a pension fund manager, but it is sensible to seek guidance on whether a pension plan will meet your future needs and whether your planning is adequate.

Summary

This chapter has outlined a simple system to manage equity allocation within the portfolio that limits the risk of loss and helps to maximise long-term returns.

The portfolio allocation rules ensure that no more than 5% of the portfolio value is invested in a single company when the portfolio value is over £20,000. For small portfolios, trading size is fixed at £1,000 to keep trading costs small relative to the portfolio size. No more than 20% of the portfolio value can be invested in any one sector at any point in time.

An investment in any individual company should never risk more than 2% of the portfolio value. No more than 15% of the overall portfolio may be at risk of loss at any point in time. For large portfolios the position and portfolio risk are decreased in order to ensure a more diverse portfolio of companies.

You should aim to invest in a portfolio of companies with a broad regional diversification of sales across developed markets. This helps to better protect from regional risks or disasters. This may prove difficult for small portfolios since you will likely be focusing on a single regional market, such as the UK, to start with, so as to keep costs down.

However, once the portfolio grows to a sufficient size it becomes cost effective to research companies in alternative regions, which will help broaden the level of regional diversification. It is useful to monitor the regional sales exposure of the portfolio to know where the biggest regional risks lie.

The rules for selling provide a natural opportunity to rebalance the portfolio and ensure it remains diversified. Rebalancing tends to improve returns as it shifts the portfolio away from expensive companies with weakening price momentum and towards companies offering better value and higher returns on average. It also allows you to take advantage of tax allowances and move money into the most appropriate investment accounts.

You should try to make full use of the tax allowances available. In the UK, this includes allowances for ISAs, capital gains, dividends and pensions. Married couples should look to hold assets jointly to make full use of both individuals' tax allowances. Making the best use of your tax allowance will help to minimise your tax bill and maximise net portfolio returns.

CHAPTER 16

BRINGING IT ALL TOGETHER

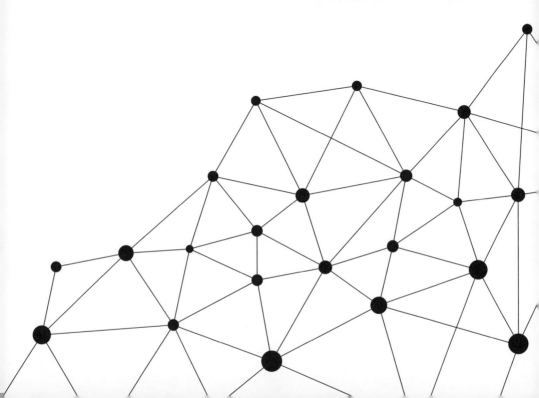

Introduction

THE PREVIOUS CHAPTERS have provided all the information needed to successfully run a long-only stocks and shares portfolio. It has outlined how to research shares to ensure their high quality and value, how to time share purchases, when to sell and how to manage your portfolio effectively.

This chapter discusses the day-to-day running of the system and how I apply it to the share portfolios I control. It is hoped that this will help you gain an improved understanding of how you could run your own portfolio.

Weekly routine

Saturday

My weekly investing routine starts early on Saturday morning.

Review current holdings (20 minutes)

I start by reviewing current holdings in the portfolio. I look at the closing share price for each company and compare it to the assigned stop loss (determined in chapter 14).

If the end of week closing price is below the assigned stop loss, the holding will be sold Monday morning. If the closing price has risen, I check to see if the stop loss should be raised to lock in profit (again, using the rules outlined in chapter 14). Where the closing share price for a company is above but close to the stop loss, this is noted and monitored closely over the following week.

Market and sector direction (20 minutes)

The next step is to look at where the market is in the price cycle. If the underlying market is in a strong, stage 4 downtrend (as described in chapter 13), no further investment in the market will be made until the trend starts to move sideways (forming a stage 1 bottom) or until the price starts to trend upwards (moving into a stage 2 recovery phase). It is also useful to note key support and resistance levels, which can help to identify potential price levels where markets tend to reverse.

If the price cycle is not in a stage 4 downtrend, a look at the underlying price direction of the market sector is then undertaken. This helps to identify which sectors are performing poorly and which are doing well. Sectors that exhibit strong downtrends in overall price are out of favour and should be avoided until improving price momentum is evident.

Conversely, sectors that exhibit strong uptrends in overall price and have positive price momentum across the sector are in favour. This should be supportive of share prices for companies in the sector, provided valuation metrics don't look too stretched. When researching companies, I try to focus on those that lie in sectors with positive price momentum, as this can offer short-term uplift to company share prices. This means that investments tend to move into profit quicker than they might otherwise do.

In addition to identifying new companies to research and invest in, I look closely at companies that have already been invested in which lie in poorly performing sectors. Such a downturn may signal a change in fundamental drivers which will hamper performance of companies in the sector. This warrants further investigation into the underlying cause of the decline and research into whether the fundamentals have deteriorated enough to trigger a sale of company shares in the sector.

Screening for stocks (30 minutes)

On the last Saturday of the month, I re-run the stock screens outlined in chapter 2. Watch lists for income, value and growth shares are created. These companies remain the focus of research for the month.

For income and value companies, I use an adjusted income summary sheet (see figure 16.1) which allows me to sort the companies by stock rank while having key information on income displayed.

The stock rank combines momentum, quality and value characteristics to provide a composite score that reflects their rank against the universe of shares. This helps provide the order to research new companies in detail, as companies with a higher stock rank have a higher likelihood of medium-term capital appreciation (i.e., share price rises). I look to research one or two companies each week from this list.

Figure 16.1 Income watch list on Stockopedia's portfolio section

Ticker	Name	Yield %	Yield % Rolling 1y	Yield % 5y Avg	Div Cover	Div Cover Rolling	Piotroski F-Score	DPS 5y CAGR %	DPS Increases	Stock Rank™	QV Rank	Quality Rank	Value Rank	Gearing %	
DEB	Debenhams	4.40	4.57	3.93	2.24	2.23	9	-	3.00	99	96	84	89	37.5	⚙ -
HEAD	Headlam	3.73	4.10	4.42	1.64	1.65	7	9.73	7.00	97	91	90	70	-14.5	⚙ -
SPRP	Sprue Aegis	2.86	4.03	0.53	3.44	2.17	6	74.1	5.00	95	94	94	74	-87.7	⚙ -
BDEV	Barratt Developments	2.60	5.79	1.10	2.95	2.10	7	-	3.00	94	83	91	53	-5.24	⚙ -
XPP	XP Power	5.75	4.48	4.17	1.14	1.52	6	22.6	9.00	92	85	95	53	0.49	⚙ -

In addition to researching companies currently on the screen, I take note of companies that were bought and have subsequently come off the previous month's watch list. I try to understand why a company is no longer on the watch list and research whether the fundamentals of the company have changed. If the fundamentals have deteriorated, I may look to tighten the stop or sell my holding in the company.

I perform a similar analysis for growth companies. In this case, I use the quality summary to sort companies by quality rank (see figure 16.2). This combines factors reflecting quality (such as profitability, cash flow and stability) to rank companies in the market universe, assigning a score between 0 and 100 with a higher score indicating a higher level of quality.

Companies with higher quality scores are given priority for research. The reason behind this is that investing in high-quality companies with high earnings growth is normally preferable to investing in high-growth companies that are of low quality. In addition, high-quality companies are more likely to pass the fundamental number checks.

Figure 16.2 Growth watch list on Stockopedia's portfolio section

	Ticker	Name	Quality Rank▾	ROCE %	ROE %	ROE % 5y Avg	Op Mgn %	Gross Mgn %	Piotroski F-Score	Altman Z Score (1)	Gearing %	Beneish M Score	Cash / Assets	Magic Formula Rank %	
☐	JUP	Jupiter Fund Management	99	34.0	28.9	15.3	48.5	80.4	8	7.06	-46.1	-1.51	32.0	-	⚙-
☐	ABBY	Abbey	97	21.5	20.5	8.69	27.9	31.4	8	7.10	-34.5	-2.21	29.1	86.8	⚙-
☐	RYA	Ryanair Holdings	97	15.2	33.7	17.5	22.3	43.7	8	3.20	-21.5	-2.65	43.8	72.5	⚙-
☐	EZJ	easyJet	96	22.5	24.8	19.2	14.7	43.8	7	3.28	-19.3	-2.53	19.4	78.8	⚙-
☐	HHPD	Hon Hai Precision Industry Co	96	13.8	16.4	15.6	3.69	7.21	8	3.40	-42.0	-2.77	29.8	82.8	⚙-
☐	QQ.	Qinetiq	93	33.1	40.9	14.7	14.3	-	7	3.85	-64.1	-	26.2	81.5	⚙-
☐	BDEV	Barratt Developments	91	12.8	12.8	5.31	15.3	19.0	7	4.01	-5.24	-1.68	6.27	74.0	⚙-

Sunday

Reading and research – Financial news (less than two hours)

On Sunday morning, I read the Sunday papers and news wires. The newspapers I look through include the *Financial Times*, the *Telegraph*, the *Sunday Times* and *The Economist*.

I focus on the broader economics and relevant company news. In particular, I look for information that is either directly applicable to the companies owned in the portfolio or companies that may eventually be bought. Related sector information and articles about competitors are also of interest. This helps keep me up-to-date with current market sentiment as well as form a forward-looking view.

Identify company shares to potentially buy (30 minutes)

Companies that have already been researched and are a buy based on fundamentals and valuation go on the shortlist. Weekly and daily share price charts are reviewed on Sunday and the chart strategies are applied to look for potential entry points. This helps identify which company shares are setting up for purchase and should be closely monitored (and possibly bought) during the following week.

Company research (less than three hours)

On Sunday evening, a few hours are spent researching new companies from the watch list. If cash is available in the ISA account (i.e., tax-free account), the focus will be on finding new income or value companies to invest in. If ISA cash has been fully invested, my focus will turn to growth companies and how to invest available cash in my trading account.

As mentioned previously, research should be guided by stock ranking for income and value companies and quality ranking for growth companies; I select the highest ranked company on the watch list to research first.

Often research is not completed in one sitting and further research is undertaken during the week (if time allows) or the following weekend. If the company is determined to be a potential buy, it is added to the shortlist for further monitoring.

Monday to Friday

Stop losses (less than 30 minutes)

The first priority of the morning is to sell company shares that have hit their stop losses. This is normally done at 9.30am, after the stock market has been open for an hour. If the company share price is still below the stop level, the shares are sold immediately. If the price has moved above the stop level, the shares are monitored throughout the day and sold only if they again fall below the stop level.

Company share prices that were identified as being close to their stop losses are monitored during the day, with price checks at lunchtime and half an hour before the market closes (at a minimum). The TradingViews website (tradingview.com) has a stock alert feature that can send an email message when the current price falls below designated stop levels. This is used for every holding in the portfolio and is an effective way to ensure everything is tracked while I am away from the computer screen.

Financial news and magazines (30 minutes)

Lunchtime usually affords an opportunity to spend half an hour reading financial news. Looking over the markets section of the *Financial Times* provides a good overview of what markets are focusing on the short term, as well as the latest economic news to have a bearing on market direction. However, the companies' section is my favourite as it is easy to skim through to find news on holdings and companies of interest.

End-of-day review (one hour)

In the evening I review technical charts for shortlisted companies looking for the next day's set-ups (which provide opportunities to purchase company shares). I also take note of companies that are below their stop loss as well as share prices that are approaching their stop loss and need to be monitored the following day.

End-of-quarter routine

On the last weekend of the quarter I take a couple of hours to review the portfolio. This involves taking note of the current holdings, total cash in the accounts and dividends that have been paid into the account over the quarter. The holdings and cash positions are recorded in a spreadsheet.

The final thing I do is calculate the total value of the portfolio. I record this in a spreadsheet so that I can see how the portfolio value has changed over time. This allows me to keep track of portfolio performance and calculate the total returns being made.

Yearly routine

I normally take two weeks at the end of March, to coincide with the end of the accounting year, to do an extensive review of the portfolio and its holdings. I review each company in the portfolio and refresh the research undertaken previously. I check my investment thesis and ensure that the reasons for investing in each company are still valid.

This helps to tidy the portfolio as it prompts the selling companies that are performing poorly (using the qualitative selling rules in chapter 14). Also identified are companies that are performing well which may be candidates for further investment.

Conclusion

I hope this book has been informative and has inspired you to manage your own portfolio of shares. Discussion of my routine shows that it takes time to monitor and maintain a portfolio, as well as stay up-to-date with events in the market and generate new ideas for the portfolio's continued development. However, I recognise that many people might not have the time nor the inclination to spend managing a portfolio.

In this case, the supporting website (www.theequityedge.com) provides useful content to help implement the system. Similarly, the newsletter subscription service provides the necessary information to carry out the approach outlined, such as analysis of companies, complete watch lists and discussion of real portfolios being managed. The information should significantly reduce the time needed to successfully manage a portfolio.

Even if you do have the time to complete the necessary analysis and management of the portfolio, you may still find it useful to have a subscription. This is so that you can compare your own analysis to that undertaken by myself and others, which will allow you to build your expertise with confidence.

INDEX